Team TURNAROUNDS

A Playbook for Transforming Underperforming Teams

Joe Frontiera
Daniel Leidl

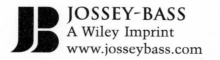

JOSSEY-BASS
A Wiley Imprint
www.josseybass.com

Published by Jossey-Bass

A Wiley Imprint

One Montgomery Street, Suite 1200, San Francisco, CA 94104-4594—www.josseybass.com

Cover design by Faceout Studio

Jossey-Bass books and products are available through most bookstores. To contact Jossey-Bass directly call our Customer Care Department within the U.S. at 800-956-7739, outside the U.S. at 317-572-3986, or fax 317-572-4002.

Wiley publishes in a variety of print and electronic formats and by print-on-demand. Some material included with standard print versions of this book may not be included in e-books or in print-on-demand. If this book refers to media such as a CD or DVD that is not included in the version you purchased, you may download this material at http:// booksupport.wiley.com. For more information about Wiley products, visit www.wiley.com.

Library of Congress Cataloging-in-Publication Data
Frontiera, Joe, 1975–
    Team turnarounds : a playbook for transforming underperforming teams / Joe Frontiera, Daniel Leidl. – First edition.
        pages cm
    Includes bibliographical references and index.
    ISBN 978-1-118-14478-7
ISBN 978-1-118-26372-3 (mobipocket) – ISBN 978-1-118-23908-7 (epub) –
ISBN 978-1-118-22574-5 (pdf)
    1. Terms in the workplace. 2. Organization. 3. Leadership. 4. Management.
I. Leidl,
Daniel, 1974– II. Title.
    HD66.F76 2012
    658.4'022–dc23

                                                                2012016807

Printed in the United States of America

FIRST EDITION

HB Printing   10 9 8 7 6 5 4 3 2 1

Contents

To our friendship,
our wives, our team

Foreword: Adversity Introduces Us to Ourselves

What do NFL teams, a Broadway musical, a university child-care center, a pizza maker, a public school system, a motorcycle trailer manufacturer, a collegiate lacrosse team, and a state all have in common? Stumped? They, and other equally fascinating organizations, are the case examples in *Team Turnarounds*, a highly entertaining and enlightening read about very diverse organizations that shared one common problem: they were all failing or floundering and needed to reverse course.

Because of the sheer breadth of their examination, it's hard to imagine how Joe Frontiera and Dan Leidl could pull this off. But they have—and to great effect. These stories are so well narrated that you'll think you're reading an edge-of-your-seat detective story. And *Team Turnarounds* really is like that in many ways. Here are tireless leaders who face severely vexing challenges and puzzling situations—many of which they and others have never before encountered. And these leaders are refreshingly honest about the realities of life in organizations that aren't performing up to expectations. That life can be embarrassing, depressing, exhausting, and heart-breaking. Yet, at the same time, it can also be exhilarating, uplifting, meaningful, and rewarding. It all depends on how you view the challenge.

While reading this book, we were reminded of a comment made by John McDonnell, former CEO of McDonnell Douglas, when that company was going through its struggles before eventually merging with Boeing. "Adversity introduces you to yourself," he said, reflecting upon what that struggle had brought for him. And we recalled another thought from Randy Melville, whom we interviewed when he was with Pepsi. Quoting his Princeton University basketball coach, Pete Carril, Randy said, "Adversity doesn't build character, it reveals it." Challenges, difficulties, setbacks, adversities—they are all familiar sights on the leadership landscape. And one of the things that they cause us to do is come face-to-face with ourselves. They are a rather harsh way of reminding us of what's important to us, what we value, and where we want to go.

Leaders are no strangers to challenges. In fact, exemplary leaders thrive on them. *Team Turnarounds* offers you the hard-earned lessons learned by the amazing people who led the transformations. And Joe and Dan have done an exemplary job of pulling these lessons together in a way that is not just applicable to the folks in the book. They show us how these lessons are applicable to all of us, and how they are especially useful during the turnarounds we are now dealing with, or will inevitably confront, in our organizations and our lives. There are lessons in here about the importance of values and visions, about commitment and meaning, about teamwork and relationships, about resilience and positivity, about initiative and commitment, and about courage and heart.

But you don't have to wait for things to get bad on your team or in your organization to benefit from Joe and Dan's insights and practical wisdom. Filled with fresh, revealing examples from sports, business, education, retail, and large and small organizations, the examples are illuminating in their depth and take-away applications. You and your entire team will benefit from the book's Team Turnaround Workbook—it alone is worth the price of the book. You'll find essential questions you must answer, tasks you must complete, and preparations you must take to successfully reverse the course of a losing team, a failing company, or a stalled initiative.

Team Turnarounds is, in the end, a book about hope. A book about how you can mobilize others to transcend the present difficulties, bounce back from failures, and reach for greatness. It's a book about the power of the human spirit. Enjoy.

March 2012

Jim Kouzes
Orinda, California
Barry Posner
Santa Clara, California

Introduction

MICHIGAN FALLING

In 2009, the state of Michigan was in a downward spiral. Statewide, it was hemorrhaging jobs, and unemployment offices were receiving 800,000 to 1,000,000 calls per day.

Governor Jennifer Granholm, then in her second term, recalled, "In our unemployment offices, people were in line down the street. [There were] people [who] had never collected unemployment before. The system was like a cancer patient that was breaking down everywhere."[1]

Granholm had reason to be concerned, and as time went on, the situation only worsened. Moreover, she had long believed that Michigan's manufacturing culture was working against the situation.

"People were so used to boom-or-bust cycles," she lamented. "They knew that historically, when the nation was in a recession, Michigan had deeper troubles because people weren't buying large consumer products, like cars."[2] And when the manufacturing industry that had once sustained Michigan's economy began failing, the shift was catastrophic, and the damage was unprecedented.

Toward the end of her first year in office, Granholm had traveled to the 8,000-person town of Greenville, Michigan, after learning that Electrolux, a refrigerator manufacturer that employed 2,700 people, had made plans to uproot its operation and move its plant to Mexico. In her typically confident way, she teamed up with the mayor, the local chamber of commerce, the company's union representatives, and others to construct a comprehensive plan to get Electrolux to stay. Granholm's team members met with executives from Electrolux and presented them with an extraordinary package, laden with concessions and incentives that they thought no business could refuse.

"We offered them zero taxes for twenty years. We offered to build them a new factory, $30 million in concessions annually, and a $750 million package over twenty years. It was the most aggressive we had ever been—that Michigan had ever been."[3]

It was a good deal, and the team members knew they had done their best to keep Electrolux in the region.

After the presentation, the Electrolux executives left the room to confer. About fifteen minutes later, they returned.

As Granholm recalled, one of the executives began, "This is really generous. We have never seen an offer like this. But," he continued, "there's nothing you can do to compensate for the fact that we can pay $1.57 an hour in Mexico, so we're moving."[4]

With that, Electrolux was gone. Electrolux had manufactured its last refrigerator in Michigan, and another Michigan community was left devastated.

Shortly afterward, the stunned citizens of Greenville held what they called a "last supper," a picnic at Klackle's Orchard Pavilion, a local indoor facility. The town was convening both to remember the past and to make sense of the present. Granholm attended the picnic.

"It was like community grieving. . . . People could not believe that their whole identity had been stripped, and not just their identity but their livelihood."[5]

One worker approached Granholm with his two young daughters. He relayed how his grandfather, his father, and he himself had all gone to work at the plant right out of high school. With his daughters looking on, he lobbed a hard question at Granholm: "So, Governor, who is going to ever hire me?" Granholm heard the emotional appeals of hundreds of families that night, all asking similar questions. She stayed until the last person left. Then she went home and cried.

Thousands of workers now needed to find a way to feed their families. Crushed though Granholm was, she also began to realize that the people of Michigan needed to change their mind-set—specifically, the ingrained belief that if they simply continued to do what they had always done, they would somehow turn things around and bring jobs back.

"We had 10 million people," she said, "and it takes a long time to get a whole cultural paradigm shift into people's mindset, and sometimes you could hit bottom before you fully acknowledge, 'Yeah, we needed to change.'"[6]

Michiganders would have to look to new industries, try new ideas, and shift the focus away from what once had worked to what could be done differently. They had to change, and they didn't have any time to waste.

TURNAROUNDS IN THE MODERN LANDSCAPE: THE TEAM TURNAROUND PROCESS

How can a governor change a culture, an ingrained belief system, in order to turn an entire state around? More broadly, how can any leader work to bring a team from the bottom to the top? This is the precise question we set out to answer as we embarked on our research project five years ago. Is it possible to transform a losing climate into one that fosters collaboration, innovation, and productivity, especially when leaders in all sectors are forced to do more with less?

We began our research in the world of professional sports, speaking with owners and general managers in the National Football League, Major League Baseball, and the National Basketball Association. Professional sports represent a unique business, where the on-field product—the team—has a hard time distancing itself from its black-and-white win-loss records. In this world, it's easy to identify a turnaround.

After our initial research was published in the 2010 *Journal of Leadership & Organizational Studies*, we expanded our questions to the world of business, talking to leaders at different levels, from CEOs to frontline managers. Some of our findings supported past research (for example, the finding that leaders at all levels, not just the highest leaders, can create change). But one amazing finding emerged. We discovered that, although the specifics of different turnarounds varied widely, and although they encompassed factors ranging from the size of the team to the scope of the challenge, there was remarkable consistency in the process that successful leaders in *all* sectors went through. We found six elements that were common to all the turnarounds we explored. These elements fit naturally into a six-stage model, one that we call the Team Turnaround Process, as shown in the following illustration.

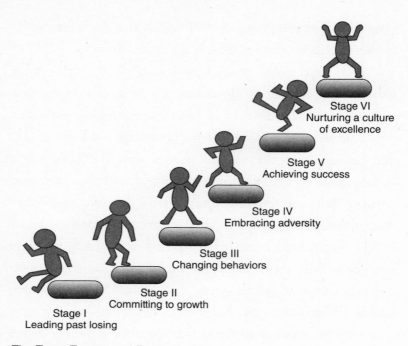

Stage VI
Nurturing a culture
of excellence

Stage V
Achieving success

Stage IV
Embracing adversity

Stage III
Changing behaviors

Stage II
Committing to growth

Stage I
Leading past losing

The Team Turnaround Process

Stage I, shown at the bottom of the illustration, is when a leader first observes the wreckage, the poor performance, and the other dynamics that are common in losing teams. Stage VI, represented at the top of the illustration, shows a team that has successfully changed and is striving to continually nurture a high-performing culture. Together, the six stages of the Team Turnaround Process form the larger developmental journey that teams go through as they move from failure to success.

Each stage contains specific developmental milestones—principles that leaders and their teams typically master before proceeding to the next stage. Most teams tend to complete a stage before moving on to the next, but you should expect occasional overlap and possibly backward cycling. Every team is unique, and even though the Team Turnaround Process captures helpful generalities, it's not intended to address all situations and scenarios.

The goal of this book is to empower you to believe that you can make positive changes. Each of the first six chapters is dedicated to a particular stage of the Team Turnaround Process and explores various elements specific to that stage, through the words and stories of executives, coaches, and leaders who have turned their organizations around. The final chapter is a hands-on workbook that offers discussion questions and exercises to further facilitate your own Team Turnaround Process. As you read through the chapters, you will discover a clear and accessible model—a playbook—for how a turnaround takes place, a model that will help you and anyone else who is intent on turning a team around. There will always be factors outside your control, but as a leader, you will find that there is plenty within your control. The stories used to capture the Team Turnaround Process will remind you of that.

OVERVIEW OF THE CHAPTERS

Stage I: Leading Past Losing

In the first stage of turning your team around, you must honestly evaluate the current state of affairs. You're not where you want to be. You may be losing games or sales, but either way, you're underperforming.

In Chapter One, Philadelphia Eagles owner Jeffrey Lurie, Kendon Industries president Frank Esposito, and Juniper Networks vice president David Helfer all discuss what they saw when they began leading their respective teams. They describe how they communicated those truths to their groups and how they slowly took action to clarify misunderstood roles and responsibilities. Stage I is the starting point, and it focuses on conducting honest evaluation, accepting the reasons for recent failures, and identifying the root causes of problems.

Stage II: Committing to Growth

Accepting reality is vital to beginning the turnaround process, but seeing past the current reality is just as important. Whereas stage I is about hard times in the past and the present, stage II is about envisioning the future. In stage II, you have a distinct opportunity to describe what the future can be and to communicate that message through a vision. The values that will guide the group forward and the plans and goals needed to focus the group on continual growth are just as important as a clear vision for the future.

In Chapter Two, Bill Polian, former president of the Indianapolis Colts; Jim Grundberg, co-owner of the SeeMore Putter Company (SeeMore Putters), a small golf-related business; and Jere Harris, co–lead producer of the Broadway musical *Spider-Man: Turn Off the Dark*, all talk about how they got a group to believe it could be better than it was. You can begin the slow shift of turning your organization toward brighter days by telling your team members that you are all going to climb upward by introducing a unique set of values, and by clarifying goals for the group to commit to.

Stage III: Changing Behaviors

In the third stage of the turnaround process, the emphasis shifts from planning the future to actual doing. Throughout this stage, leaders introduce new behaviors and best practices, and they slowly work to reinforce them.

In Chapter Three, Ani Shabazian, director of a child care center; Marilyn Masaitis, owner of a diner; and Kim Mulkey, coach of a national championship women's basketball team, tell their stories of how their organizations learned new behaviors, how those behaviors were modeled, and, ultimately, how celebration and discipline were used to reinforce champion-level efforts and action.

Stage IV: Embracing Adversity

Once you and your team have adopted the behaviors needed for success, you'll be ready to go out and test yourselves. As your team slowly turns around, it will inevitably face roadblocks, but these challenges can prove beneficial. Your team will grow stronger by meeting them head on and overcoming them.

As you will see in Chapter Four, Tim McIntyre, Russell Weiner, and Patrick Doyle, key members of the executive team at Domino's Pizza; and Bill Stoneman, former general manager of the Los Angeles Angels of Anaheim, used challenges to create resilient, positive, and confident teams. In stage IV, challenges are embraced, and your team begins to feed off obstacles as a means of testing its strength and becoming even stronger.

Stage V: Achieving Success

In stage V, you will finally meet with success. Your team will have identified where it wants to go, taken the steps to get there, and proved it's a contender by overcoming challenges. Your team will now be ready to win.

This is a stage filled with achievement, but the team's accomplishments are also accompanied by the logical question *What's next?* Once you've achieved your goals, where do you go? How do you recalibrate and move on?

Chapter Five—which features an inspiring definition of success offered by Mike Daly, coach of a national championship lacrosse team, along with a unique description of adaptation provided by Matt Kopac, an intriguing executive at a small e-mail-based marketing firm—will help you come to view a win as marking less of an end than a beginning.

Stage VI: Nurturing a Culture of Excellence

The final stage in our model serves as the foundation for future success. As your team evolves into stage VI, it will continue to succeed, but now sustainability becomes the focus. As you turn your attention to sustaining the organization's progress, you will place an explicit focus on three principles that have actually been with you since stage I of the Team Turnaround Process; continual learning and innovation, along with an intense understanding and maintenance of your culture, will take center stage.

By stage VI, your team will have become a winning machine, but maintaining a dynasty requires a constant effort to stay out in front and continually grow. In Chapter Six, you will hear from Dan Rooney, owner of what is arguably the most successful franchise in the National Football League (NFL), and from Jerry Weast, recently retired superintendent of a large Maryland public school district. Both share their insights into continual achievement and explain the importance of always learning and innovating, and of nurturing a culture of excellence.

Chapter Seven, the final chapter, is a practical workbook designed to help you lead your team through the Team

Turnaround Process. In Chapter Seven, leaders will find a number of exercises intended to help bring clarity to their own thoughts and to the team's internal processes. Other exercises are designed to help a team expand its overall awareness. The exercises in the workbook are organized to fit within one of the six stages of the Team Turnaround Process. Depending upon where your team is in the process, you can easily identify exercises within the appropriate stage to help your team move forward.

MICHIGAN RISING

For Michigan, the bottom came in 2009, but that low point was preceded by a chain of events far outside the control of Michigan's governor. The subprime mortgage crisis had hit in 2007, collapsing the inflated housing bubble. A global energy crisis followed and drove gas prices to their peak of well over $4 per gallon in the summer of 2008. Michigan's Big Three auto companies—Chrysler, Ford, and GM—saw their sales plummet; at the end of April 2009, Chrysler declared bankruptcy, and a month later GM followed suit. The entire American auto industry, which Michigan so heavily relied upon, came to a screeching halt. As Granholm recalled, "We had thousands of supplier businesses that feed into the auto industry. When [the Big Three] imploded, the ripple effect was just unbelievable."[7] Layoffs soon followed, jobless claims increased, and the government's ability to respond to this onslaught was compromised because of the reduced revenue from state income taxes.

Granholm told business leaders at the time, "We cannot allow ourselves to be buffeted by the winds of this global hurricane. We have to steer into it and become the change that we have most feared."[8] She conducted a careful examination of Michigan's history, and of the resources that the state provided by virtue of its blue-collar workforce and its geography, and she developed a plan that identified six future industries—life sciences, advanced manufacturing, clean energy, film, tourism, and homeland security/defense—that could help to diversify Michigan's auto-reliant economy. She set specific goals to increase the educational level of Michigan's workers and to double the number of college graduates. She established policies (such as "No Worker Left Behind") that aligned with those goals and allowed unemployed workers two years of free college education, provided that they studied for jobs in one of the six future industries. She also went overseas and aggressively brought jobs back home to Michigan because, as she said, "instead of allowing ourselves to be victimized by the globe, we need to take advantage of it."[9] Granholm resolved to turn Michigan and its economy around. Once she understood what needed to be done, she gave it all she had.

For Granholm, the implosion of the auto industry may have represented rock bottom, but it also provided a rallying point. "This is Michigan's crucible," Granholm said, but she also asserted with conviction that the state was "going to come out stronger and more resilient" because of it.[10]

In 2008, as the crisis gained steam, the Pew Center on the States rated Michigan among the top three best-managed states in the country. Susan Urahn, managing director of the organization, said at the time, "The governor has not, as she says, 'wasted the opportunity of a crisis.' Michigan has used a strategic, statewide plan to ensure that the state's critical work for the public gets done—in spite of a battered manufacturing sector that has affected state revenue."[11] Ultimately, Granholm was largely successful in leading the state through change. Even if it was slow, the turnaround was happening.

Unemployment peaked at 14.5 percent during the auto crisis. But when Granholm left office, on January 1, 2011, the unemployment rate had fallen to 10.7 percent. Michigan led the nation in Gallup's Job Creation Index for 2009–2010.[12] In addition, Granholm is credited with creating 653,000 jobs in the state of Michigan during her tenure.[13] She also left her successor with a $600 million surplus, and she left the state with the best technological infrastructure in government.[14]

The change in Michigan may be incomplete, but the way in which the state has progressed is reflective of the Team Turnaround Process. All the Team Turnaround Process needs is one leader to see the truth, identify where things have gone wrong, and broadcast the reality that losing is both unnecessary and not good enough. At that point, the turnaround journey begins.

By no means does Jennifer Granholm think the job in Michigan is complete. Her tenure was subject to Michigan's term-limit law, but she is adamant that "there still needs to be a continuous blasting of the wake-up call in Michigan to this day because there's still a lot of people who have not bought into the fact that they themselves have got to change."[15] Granholm's term as governor has ended, but her legacy and her larger message of continual progress will live on.

Leading a losing team to success is difficult, and there will be setbacks, but there's no end to the success you can achieve if you push your team to grow, challenge itself, and be better while keeping its focus on what's possible in spite of what's actually happening. Big wins never come easy, and success is a process with no end, but if you keep working through the Team Turnaround Process, victory is inevitable.

Stage I: Leading Past Losing

Organizations in stage I are at the bottom. For those who are guiding organizations at this early stage, the diagnosis is obvious. Your team is failing as you consistently and unequivocally lose games, customers, profits, and credibility. And losing can become a comfortable norm that team members cling to, accepting poor performance because winning simply isn't seen as possible.

To the outside world, such organizations appear to be hopeless case studies of bad decision making, poor management, and weak execution. Internally, the destructive dynamics are crippling. Resources are scarce, attitudes and teamwork are abysmal, the willingness to accept failure is often trumped by convenient rationalizations and denial, and roles and responsibilities are both unclear and mismatched.

Although organizations in stage I are largely defined by all they do wrong, they are full of promise. As you guide your group through this early stage, there has to be a distinct and narrow focus on understanding the team's losing ways. Observation and reflection are the keys to moving forward, and you are charged with asking questions, discerning the truth, and accepting the answers. Working to understand why the team is losing is the goal, and exploration and examination are critical.

Stage I is an investigation into why your organization is performing poorly. It's a time for neither judgment nor decisive action, but it's critical that a foundation for growth be laid. Throughout this stage, you are building a clear case for why changes need to occur and for what those changes should be. You should be prepared to gather evidence regarding where your organization is missing the mark, and regarding what a winning organization does differently. You also need to identify just how team members can be shifted into roles that best suit their skills.

Although making the case for needed change may seem like a straightforward endeavor, don't lose sight of the current state of the team. An organization in stage I has been beaten and battered, and the hope of an optimistic and honest leader is critical. Ultimately, the leader of a failing organization not only has to understand why the team continues to fall flat but also must be able to revitalize the dejected team by creating a light at the end of the tunnel, and pointing to where the group can go. To do this, it's necessary to study and define success. By studying industry success stories, drawing on the more personal and individual successes, and talking with people who have led high-achieving teams, you can better identify what the group should be striving for.

To help you better understand stage I, we will explore the experiences of three leaders who walked into failing teams with the goal of identifying what was going wrong. Jeffrey Lurie purchased the Philadelphia Eagles in 1994 for a record sum, only to spend the better part of his early years as owner trying to uncover the problems that kept the franchise from winning. Similarly, Frank Esposito brought years of experience in the motorcycle trailer industry to Kendon Industries, not only determined to uncover where the small company was failing but also committed to communicating the truth to the desperate team. And David Helfer moved halfway around the world to study how the Europe, Middle East, and Africa territory of Juniper Networks could operate more efficiently and effectively, focusing much of his energy on identifying the roles and responsibilities best suited to particular team members. All three of these teams were struggling, underperforming groups with far more potential than their achievements indicated. Their turnarounds began with patient and curious leaders who were determined to uncover what was wrong while instilling the belief that things would eventually become right.

OBSERVE AND LEARN

Organizations that are losing know it. The profits aren't there, customers are absent, quality is cheap, and the brand isn't trusted. Yet acknowledging failure is painful and difficult, even though all the facts may suggest that the team is underperforming. Starting the turnaround process begins with recognizing and highlighting the group's losses and shortcomings, but it requires the skill of a patient and determined leader. For an organization to begin the turnaround process, the leader has to observe the team, learn where the failures lie, and then expose those failures. One team that knows this process all too well is the Philadelphia Eagles. It took the help of Jeffrey Lurie, a Hollywood producer with a Ph.D. in social policy, to get the organization to see what was wrong before it could turn itself around.

Teams in the National Football League don't come up for sale often, and so prospective buyers are in the unenviable position of taking whatever they can get. In 1994, when Lurie decided to buy the Philadelphia Eagles for $185 million—the highest price ever paid for a sports franchise up to that point— he knew that the team had underperformed over the previous decade. The team was coming off a 1994 season in which it had logged 7 wins and 9 losses, and over the previous twelve seasons (1982–1993) the team had accumulated a record that barely topped .500, at 100 wins and 98 losses. In the same twelve years, the Eagles advanced to the playoffs only four times, winning only one playoff game out of the five it played.

Given the team's on-field performance, Lurie knew he was buying a franchise that was accustomed to mediocrity. What he didn't know was that the organizational problems extended far beyond actual wins and losses. Not only did Lurie spend a record amount of cash on the ailing Eagles, he also bought the team sight unseen. Once he saw what he had bought, the extent of the franchise's issues quickly became apparent.

"I'll always remember the day I actually bought the team, the facilities, sight unseen," Lurie says, "I mean, I knew about Veterans Stadium, but I really didn't know about the working conditions of the employees. It was startling and depressing, the first few months, to be in an environment where there are no windows."

To Lurie's credit, he didn't freak out or let the depression overwhelm him. He moved forward, exploring and cataloging what wasn't working and what might have to change, and eventually studying the ways of winning franchises in an effort to understand more successful organizations.

One of the primary concerns for Lurie was the facilities. The Eagles operated and played out of Veterans Stadium, a Philadelphia landmark that had slowly decayed into a relic of the good old days. The stadium had its appeal as a "time portal" capable of whisking fans back to its 1971 grand opening, but it had serious flaws as a professional sports arena and operations home for an NFL franchise. For Eagles employees other than the players, the Vet had become an awful place to work. The dingy lighting, the basement-level work area, the broken elevator, the rumors and fears of rats, and the windowless offices were depressing morale busters. For the players and the coaching staff, the cramped quarters made it nearly impossible to interact, and there wasn't a single room in the facility where the entire team could meet to discuss strategy or where team members could just get to know one another. And for the fans, watching a game at the stadium was disruptive and uncomfortable. According to Lurie, "The sight lines for fans, which are the first thing I always kind of look at when I go into a stadium, were so distant! It was one of those multipurpose stadiums that was poor for football and poor for baseball." Suffice it to say, employees didn't enjoy their time working inside the stadium, and the fans weren't excited about watching games from the stands. Lurie took note, continued cataloging the Vet's limitations, and waited.

As real as the issues at Veterans Stadium were, the problems with the organization were far more complicated than poor sight lines and a few rats. But the stadium was an easy target. It couldn't get offended, argue, or react to the criticism, and its failures were shared by everyone. Nevertheless, as Lurie continued to explore what was keeping the Eagles from succeeding, he started to look past bricks and mortar and deeper into the dynamics of the actual team. What Lurie began to find was not unexpected, but it was unsettling.

Championship teams often share a distinct collection of characteristics. Losing teams do, too. Patrick Lencioni, a leadership expert, defines the five characteristics of a poorly performing team as *absence of trust, fear of conflict, lack of commitment, avoidance of accountability,* and *inattention to results.* Lencioni suggests that each of these characteristics works to deteriorate the effectiveness of the team, promoting dysfunction and ultimately failure. For example, if two individuals don't trust one another, they will be "incapable of engaging in a debate of ideas," and this shortcoming will inevitably compromise the quality of the ideas developed.[1]

The Eagles seemed to model Lencioni's five dysfunctions. Communication was poor, and trust was nonexistent. Healthy conflict didn't take place, and team members lacked commitment to each other, to the fans, and to the organization. There was little accountability, and the team's win-loss record was evidence enough that the franchise may not have been placing much attention on results. But what Lurie noted was the attitude of the office staff. He observed the staff and concluded that there "wasn't a lot of excitement or enthusiasm." Staff members just came to work, did their thing, and went home. They weren't bringing passion to their jobs, and Lurie noticed.

He explored further, watching the departments and personnel interact, and concluded that there was "clearly a large wall between the football operations and the business operations, or the rest of the operation." There was no unity and there was no shared purpose. Each camp fought for itself, blaming the other camp for failures and mistakes. If the team was losing, it was the football side's fault, which led to poor ticket sales and anger on the business side of the organization. If the business side didn't fill the house, the football operations wondered how any team could perform with a weak crowd.

The two sides pointed fingers at each other and wouldn't cooperate to solve the problems.

As Lurie continued to watch and gather information, he unearthed more and more types of behaviors and interactions that would have been destructive to the success of any team.

"It seemed very contentious," he says. "It was sort of epitomized by the equipment manager, who had a very negative view of players and was very reluctant to issue socks and hand warmers."

The equipment manager thought that the players were asking for such items in order to steal them. And this questioning of the players' requests for warm clothes, in the cold Philadelphia climate, was just one of many ways in which mistrust within the organization manifested. On the surface, the issue of hoarding socks—because of the fear that millionaires were going to steal them—may seem childish. But Lurie came to associate this type of exchange as reflective of a much larger problem. Regardless of who was right, it was indicative of the much more serious issue of pervasive negativity, which couldn't coexist with winning championships. Essentially, this type of mistrust and selfishness can spread like a virus, infecting one person after another and eventually bringing the whole organization down. Individuals have the potential to be "walking mood inductors."[2] As such, they can exert an impact on the emotions, the judgments, and even the behaviors of other individuals and groups. For Lurie, the Eagles were fighting an illness that had permeated the whole organization, and the dysfunctional interactions were symptoms of an unhealthy culture.

"I felt like the biggest challenge, by far," he says, "was changing the culture to one where you expect to be very good and proud of your franchise, both on the field and in the community."

Lurie had seen enough. After collecting information about what was wrong, he set out to establish a blueprint for correcting the problems. He wanted to sell the organization on what it could be, on where it could go, and what hard work and focus could lead to, but first he had to paint a picture of what success was. He knew that between 1981 and 1994 the San Francisco 49ers had been among the most dominant teams in the NFL. Out of a sixteen-game season, the franchise had won ten or more games every year but one (the 1982 season had been shortened to nine games because of a strike). The 49ers had missed the playoffs only once, and they had reeled in five Super Bowl championships. As a new owner, Lurie was intrigued. He wanted to study success, and the 49ers were as successful as any team going. He reached out to San Francisco and asked if he could meet Bill Walsh, the 49ers' head coach from 1979 through 1988. Walsh, who died in 2007, was largely credited as the architect of the 49ers' dynasty, and Lurie knew that Walsh would have plenty of insights into what makes a franchise good.

"I spent a lot of time with Bill Walsh and those guys out there because I admired them," says Lurie. "During the first six months of owning the team, I spent more time with those guys than anyone else, just because I admired what they had done, the culture, the expectation to be very good. I wanted to understand the approach they took to their own players, their employees, and their scouting systems, and I had a feeling that they did want to be the best, and recognized that they were the best."

Lurie considers talking with the 49ers a critical point in his development as an owner, but it was also a critical point in the Eagles' eventual turnaround. Not only did Lurie keep tabs on what would have to change within the Eagles franchise, he also went out of house to take a look at what a winning organization does. In so doing, Lurie built a case for what would have to change with the Eagles, why it would have to change, and how it would eventually have to change.

In this early period of turning an organization around, a leader simply has to take stock of what's wrong. Lurie began by watching quietly and noting deficiencies in the facilities and the team dynamics as well as taking note of concerns with the larger culture. On the ground in Philadelphia, he attempted to understand why the organization was failing, but he also worked to define success by talking with Bill Walsh and the staff of the San Francisco 49ers. Lurie took hold of opposite ends of the performance spectrum, and he grasped the stark differences between the two. Eventually he worked to bridge the gap, but before taking action, he studied, watched, asked questions, and worked to define both what was wrong with the Eagles and what they should eventually be doing right.

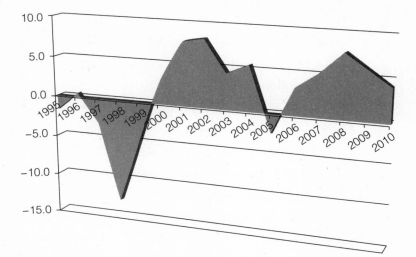

Figure 1.1. SRS for the Philadelphia Eagles, 1995–2010*
*This figure shows the Simple Rating System (SRS) as it applies to the Philadelphia Eagles from 1995 through 2010. The SRS, created by sports-reference.com, is a statistical measure of a given team's overall strength, taking into account its margin of victory and the strength of the other teams it is scheduled to play in a given year. The SRS league average is 0. Numbers greater than 0 indicate that a team's performance is stronger than the league average, whereas negative numbers indicate that a team's performance is weaker than the league average.

As Figure 1.1 shows, Lurie's early observations provided a solid foundation for the Eagles organization and ultimately led the team to success. Lurie worked hard to correct the issues he had uncovered and to significantly raise the performance standard. From 1995 to 1999, Lurie's Eagles endured three losing seasons, accruing a combined record of 34 wins and 45 losses, but he knew he wanted to build his team for long-term success, and he saw those early losses as part of the team's growth. The Eagles turned the corner in 2000 and have been one of the most dominant teams in the National Football League ever since. From 2000 through 2010, the Eagles have amassed 113 wins against only 62 losses. They have advanced to the playoffs nine times, to the NFC conference championship five times, and to the Super Bowl once. Their 2004 Super Bowl run ended in their loss of the championship game, but the Eagles have established themselves as a perennial Super Bowl contender and as a dramatically different organization from the one Lurie purchased in 1994.

FACE REALITY

Once you understand what's wrong, it's time to let the team in on the secret—to go beyond platitudes and face reality, no matter how disconcerting it may be. It's time to shine a light on all the issues that have been swept under the rug for so long, and to inform the group that the future does not need to look like the present. This process can be hard, and confronting the issues will make a lot of people uncomfortable, but it's necessary. In moving through stage I, once you've gathered information about the problem, you have to deliver that information.

When people are in denial, there's a truth out there that they are afraid to recognize consciously, something that is simply too difficult to embrace.[3] Rationalizations become tools to explain behaviors in terms that may feel good but are often used at the expense of reality. These rationalizations serve to sidestep the actual problem, ensuring that nothing really changes. This kind of thinking is debilitating, but it can be successfully confronted and changed when rationalizations and denial are exposed to an onslaught of truth.

Teams in any sort of lengthy decline become vulnerable to using rationalizations and denial as a means to explain away and ignore breakdowns.[4] Similar to an alcoholic who tells his wife he doesn't have a drinking problem while he downs a case of beer, an organization can fail to acknowledge its own decline. Members look the other way rather than acknowledge the trouble that the team or organization is in. Employees of an organization may reject the idea that a competitor's product has overtaken their own, or that they don't have the necessary skills, or that they're not prepared for the immense challenges that lie ahead. As denial and rationalizations increase, the problems that come with them grow in severity. The issues become more debilitating, and until the truth is dealt with, the organization keeps diving down.

When Frank Esposito was named president of Kendon Industries, he walked into an organization that was mired in rationalizations and denial. Kendon is a small company with around twenty-five employees in Anaheim, California. Kendon is in the business of manufacturing and selling motorcycle lifts and trailers, and at one point these products were among the best in their field. Kendon was once an industry darling, but eventually the company fell from grace while chasing the promise of quick growth and million-dollar profits. As a niche organization producing a specialty product, Kendon had been turning heads with eye-popping designs as well as high-end quality and service. But, as Esposito explains, the company bought into a faulty promise. When Kendon committed to the strategy that it could build its trailers for 20 percent less, sell 50 percent more of them, and lower the price, the problems began. The culture at Kendon shifted from one of considerate, creative artisans to one of "make a lot of money, take costs out, be cheap, and get rich." Success slowly turned to frustration and failure. The industry darling hit the skids, with nothing to hold on to but unsubstantiated claims and the false promise of getting rich quick.

Production was outsourced overseas. Regional vendors were put into bidding wars and dumped as soon as cheaper labor was found. Then, when Kendon tried to enter a different market with a product that the company didn't specialize in, customers as well as distributors and vendors started asking questions. Costs were continually cut, the quality of Kendon's products began to decline, and eventually customer service began to go, too. According to Esposito, inside the company there were "a million excuses" despite declining sales, lost customers and partners, and growing criticism, and the company "basically denied that real, relevant problems even existed." Quality and profits continued to plummet. "Dealers and consumers started to get kind of fed up with the Kendon brand, which they had once loved," Esposito says. Kendon was in the throes of a dangerous downward spiral but refused to acknowledge that problems existed.

Slowly the company began to fade, and a competitor eventually emerged because Kendon couldn't mind its shop. The owners watched as their company began to tank. Profits dropped, relationships were damaged, quality was sacrificed, and employee satisfaction was gone. Kendon had hit rock bottom. Finally, and to its credit, Kendon acknowledged the truth. The company was losing badly and needed help if it wanted to stay alive.

"When they offered me the position, it was kind of a crazy phone call," Esposito explains, "because they'd already figured it out. They were losing money, and they were watching the company that they'd built crumble. I didn't have to convince them that they had a problem," he adds. "They knew."

Kendon had been spiraling downward, but eventually the company had the presence of mind to face facts and reach out for help.

Webs of deceit are woven from uncomfortable pressures and conflicting demands. Lies and denial, rationalizations and untruths, are not born of comfortable situations. Deceit requires extra energy because the lies have to be dealt with through a variety of rationalizations. Beyond the internal conflicts and inefficiencies that rise out of a deceitful culture, there are external ramifications of the internal lies, and these consequences aren't rosy, either. An organization that can't embrace the facts about its performance runs the risk of sacrificing its reputation as well as its relationships with external constituents.[5]

But the funny thing about the truth is that people often *want* to embrace it. They may not want to hear it, but once it's spoken, everyone's shoulders drop in relief. Finally, someone has noticed that the organization has been skating by. Finally, someone is willing to confront the ugly reality. Finally, someone is putting the success of the group above everything else.

At Kendon, Esposito had the personality to match the task. Candid and forthright, Esposito doesn't come across as one who is able to skirt the truth. In January 2009, when he came in to right the ship, he started strengthening the organization's weak sense of reality by taking a more objective approach.

"I'm a validator," he says, "I don't just grab my own opinion and run with it. I go validate things pretty thoroughly."

He started by interviewing the team members, asking them about the direction of the company, where it was going, what needed fixing, and what needed to be changed. For the first time in a long while, Kendon had someone who was going to rely on facts and seek proof. No longer would the group be vulnerable to easy rationalizations and convenient denials.

What may have been most stunning for Esposito in those early efforts was his discovery that denial seemed to permeate the organization but didn't reside in individual employees.

When they were given the opportunity to share their opinions, the employees clearly weren't satisfied with poor quality.

"The very common answer," Esposito says, "was that they wanted to be proud of the product, and they wanted to take their time and build the best. They were instructed not to do that."

The individual employees wanted to be craftsmen, delivering a high-end product with passion and care, but the company had outsourced production and cut corners in a chase for profits that had compromised Kendon's very foundation. Sadly, until Esposito got the employees talking, the truth was being silenced, and the company was working itself into extinction.

"They knew what the problems were," Esposito explains, "but they were just helpless, and their voices were muffled, or they were hobbled. People literally got reprimanded or put in their place for speaking up. So they gave up."

In time, the truth was not only suppressed, it was discouraged. In short, not only had Kendon lost the truth, it had also lost one of its most prized assets—the passion of its employees.

When employees lack motivation, engagement, and the belief that they can positively impact their team, two sets of expectations are likely to develop. There are the spoken expectations, or stated goals, and then there are the shadow expectations, or shared goals that have developed informally between team members and that are considerably less rigorous than the stated goals.[6] People know that they have to publicly shoot for the spoken expectations, but most of them have their eyes on the shadow expectations, which are much lower. After all, the members of the team have learned that they're not capable of achieving the stated goals, and so there's no use in trying if their efforts can't get them where they want to go. This stance is typical of the attitude known as "learned helplessness."[7]

"When I first got here," Esposito says, "the culture was just very lifeless, very slow-paced. People just didn't care. They were moving slowly, ignoring things. Again, they were trained, kind of like a dog slapped with a hand. The next hand that reaches out, to pet it—the dog still shrinks away."

The Kendon employees had given up. Esposito describes this phenomenon, trying to make sense of a sad and confusing situation.

"They'd had the roller-coaster ride of the early days, of everything being done right, and a tremendous amount of pride," he says, but they had been "knocked down to the point where it was literally just a job, and just being paid for attendance, and 'I'll do the minimum amount and just get my paycheck, and nothing I say matters.'"

The employees had literally learned helplessness. They couldn't see how their efforts might stop the company from failing. The false promise of big payouts had trumped the value of honest feedback, and the employees eventually gave up trying. Why try when nothing you do matters? Instead, they put their energy into coping and getting by as opposed to working with creativity and productivity, and the results proved disastrous.

It's taken a few years, but things are changing. Relationships with the top two distributors in the motorcycle industry have been restored, a performance-based pay system has been instituted, manufacturing is now housed solely in the United States, and the brand has returned to its original position, focusing on quality and value.[8] As for the employees, "they believe in the company," Esposito says. "They believe in me. They haven't had raises for quite a long time. They communicate. They work with pride. The environment here—there's a sense of urgency. Problems don't sit. People talk to each other. The culture is changing."

Esposito uses caution in explaining what's happening at Kendon, acknowledging that the transformation is anything but complete. Likening the company's progress to the process of emerging from a raging river, he says, "We're still clawing up the bank." But Kendon has done away with denial and rationalizations, and hope is slowly returning.

Kendon is on a new path. With the help of Esposito, the company is working to open up communication channels, to value honest and objective feedback, and to maintain its commitment to being a niche company that makes darn good trailers and lifts. As Esposito explains, "Kendon has to be the premier brand of fold-up, stand-up, open-wheel trailers and lifts in the power-sports industry. Period."

The strategy has become very simple. Kendon has reinvested in some basic principles and is focused on designing, building, and selling the very best products it can. The company has patched up relationships with vendors, refocused on customer relationships, and is spending more time on building relationships internally. Kendon has gone back to its roots, and back to what works. The company has divested itself of deceit and invested in hard work, and it seems more comfortable being a small company that can focus on product integrity and slow, measured growth.

At this stage of the Team Turnaround Process, the truth is an antidote. It wakes up zombielike employees who have been dealing with failure simply because they have seen no other way. Confronting employees with the facts of long-term losses reminds them that their jobs matter. When a leader says that the current standard of achievement is unacceptable, people often become excited with the possibility of a new standard and charged up by the passion of a leader who actually cares. For Frank Esposito and Kendon Industries, the truth was a lifeline. Kendon is slowly coming back, but only because it accepted the truth.

DEFINE ROLES AND RESPONSIBILITIES

Role clarity is vital for success in any organization, but teams in stage I lack it. Without clear roles and responsibilities, team members lose focus and motivation and are left to wallow in mediocrity. Individuals who are insecure about what they should do and how they should do it are often reluctant to do anything. As role ambiguity increases, job satisfaction and influence decrease, anxiety grows, and performance and confidence decline.[9,10]

Clearly defined roles give employees a level of stability and promote more focused and more productive efforts. In guiding teams through stage I, it is imperative that leaders identify necessary responsibilities and define clear roles for team members. Nevertheless, as with all the other components of this initial stage of turning a poorly performing team around, leaders must first gather information.

Juniper Networks is headquartered in Sunnyvale, California, and posted more than $4 billion in revenue in 2010. The company, a leading innovator in network technology and solutions, offers products that range from mobile infrastructure to a network operating system that promises to decrease network operating costs by up to 41 percent. David Helfer is vice president of partners for the Europe, Middle East, and Africa (EMEA) territory of Juniper Networks. Stationed in London, Helfer is a long way from his hometown of East Lansing, Michigan, but he was sent there from Juniper's Silicon Valley headquarters with the distinct purpose of turning the partner (channel) team around.

When Helfer first took his position, he observed that his team was spending time and energy developing relationships with the wrong people. A partner team is supposed to facilitate the sale of its product by other, oftentimes larger, organizations, thereby leveraging an existing sales channel. But Juniper's EMEA team was selling directly to smaller clients.

The team's approach reduced the overall sales potential and had a significant impact on productivity.

As Helfer began the task of turning the team around, much of his early attention centered on better understanding individual roles and responsibilities. One of his first tasks was to identify the jobs that people were actually doing, in contrast to where they best fit.

"There was a real lack of consistency," he says. "You had partner account managers throughout EMEA, and many of them had different compensation plans. They had different targets, they had different objectives, they had different titles, they had different responsibilities. People were moving forward and trying to do the right thing, but not necessarily in a cohesive strategy."

In other words, Helfer walked into a team that had great intentions, worked hard, and was incredibly skilled, but many of its people weren't in the right places. He had punters acting as quarterbacks and outfielders pitching. The roles had to be reordered and realigned, but first Helfer needed to identify where people were best suited to help the team.

Throughout his life, Helfer has played for winning as well as losing teams. He's been a superstar and a benchwarmer and seems equally excited about and comfortable with whatever role he has to play, if it will lead to victory. To highlight this point, he tells the story of his senior season as captain of his three-time National Collegiate Athletic Association (NCAA) championship tennis team at Kalamazoo College.

"I didn't play a single match in the NCAA finals," he says. Instead, he strung a sophomore's racquet rather than take the court. "It was a bit humbling that I was helping the team in a different way. I wanted the team to win a national championship, but I didn't play."

As captain of the team that year, Helfer was seen as a leader. He had won two consecutive NCAA titles, and his team was going for a third. But Helfer just wasn't up to snuff that year. His teammates were simply more talented.

He could have pouted or even quit, but instead he assumed a supportive role and filled in where the team needed him. Even if that meant stringing an underclassman's racquet, Helfer resigned himself to being the best captain and teammate he could be, and his efforts paid off. He captained the team to victory. Helfer may not have played in that final match, but he was an integral component of the team, and he has three NCAA rings to show for it. Needless to say, Helfer understands teamwork, and the value of embracing roles and defining responsibilities.

As Helfer worked to better understand where Juniper's EMEA team was challenged, he methodically collected facts, asked questions, and ran analyses. He made himself accessible, believing that "people don't follow titles, they follow people." He was curious and genuinely interested in what was holding his team back, and he hoped to help not only the larger group but also the individuals who were struggling.

As Helfer got deeper into his early investigation, his concern for how roles and responsibilities were being determined grew. "Probably one of the bigger things," he says, "was actually the roles individuals were playing." The right people weren't in the right places, titles weren't reflecting what needed to be done, and even the way in which relationships with partners (clients) were being determined was muddy.

Helfer explains two aspects of the EMEA team, focusing on how salespeople and account managers are key players who need to assume radically different roles.

"Our partner account managers are very good," he says. "However, their entire compensation plan, and what they were looking after, looked more like a salesperson than a partner account manager. Those are two very different, distinct roles, and you would typically apply two different skill sets to those roles."

What was happening in Juniper's EMEA territory was that there was insufficient focus on aligning skills, titles, compensation, and expectations. Instead, people were working hard and even making progress in these somewhat amorphous and oftentimes confusing roles, but for all their efforts, the territory wasn't moving forward. In other words, clarity and focus were weak, and the team was suffering.

Upon joining a team, an individual holds a belief about what his or her responsibilities and contributions should be. Similarly, an employer has expectations of what that individual will deliver. Regardless of how a role has been defined by a leader and interpreted by an employee, each of them inevitably develops a personal understanding of what that role is. This dynamic, this unstated bargain, is called a *psychological contract*.[11]

As with anything else that is unspoken, there is room for misinterpretation. If an individual takes a full-time position with the expectation of working between forty and fifty hours per week but soon finds that there is no way to complete the work in under seventy hours, that employee will likely feel that the organization is not honoring its side of the deal. This situation could lead to a feeling of being devalued, and even to the employee's acting out. The employee may start expending less effort, may become emotionally disengaged, and may even do just the bare minimum in the job. All of these reactions would be fueled by the perception that the organization is not holding up its end of the unstated bargain.

When problems with a psychological contract occur, the existing psychological contract needs to be eliminated, and a new one must take its place. To begin anew, it is necessary to outline the terms in a more explicit manner. At Juniper, Helfer put more focus on communication, even brainstorming communication strategies, such as video messaging and texting, so that he could better connect with his widely dispersed team members. He also began to ask the most critical question of all: "You ask them the simple question 'What's your job? How are you being judged and measured?' You'd be amazed sometimes at how different the answer is from what you're expecting. But that's the reason you ask it."

In asking this simple question, Helfer was uncovering the existing psychological contract, and giving himself an opportunity to adjust and clarify it. One key to a viable psychological contract is that it has to be entered into freely. By bringing to the surface and correcting employees' implicit understandings, Helfer allowed the team members to freely choose whether or not they wanted to be parties to the newly defined agreements.

When Helfer arrived in London, he joined a group of hardworking individuals mired in confusion about their individual roles and responsibilities. It was critical for Helfer to understand how roles could be made clearer, and how responsibilities could better suit individual skills. He set out to identify where roles were ambiguous and to discover what responsibilities were best matched with specific job functions. As his understanding grew, he began to help his team members understand and embrace just what their jobs actually were.

By continually working to find a common understanding, and by clearly communicating responsibilities, Helfer was eventually able to bring old assumptions to the surface and explicitly rectify any misperceptions that team members had. Once Helfer was confident that team members understood their roles and responsibilities, he knew that his team was ready to take the next step in the Team Turnaround Process.

THE PLAYBOOK FOR LEADING PAST LOSING

Underperforming teams share distinct traits. As they drop to rock bottom, they become accustomed to losing, even comfortable with it. Their resources and attitudes are deficient, and teamwork and communication are limited. They ignore the truths behind their letdowns, relying on rationalizations and denial to get from one day to the next. These teams have a poor understanding of roles. They lose motivation and fail to execute because expectations and responsibilities are unclear. Organizations at stage I are broken and in desperate need of leaders to step in and honestly appraise and acknowledge any and all shortcomings.

Stage I of the turnaround process is the critical first step toward the fulfillment of even the most unlikely of dreams. Teams at this initial stage have difficulty believing that any level of success, let alone great or historic achievement, might be possible. But this early stage is the foundation on which greatness will develop. At this initial stage, leaders are called on to find and communicate the truth of the situation. You must explore your organization, uncover all the problems, and stare down, with open eyes, the ugly reality of losing. From there, you can communicate the truth with courage, conviction, and skill to the rest of the team.

The truth will often come as a relief to team members, but embracing the faults and flaws of the organization is still an uncomfortable and sometimes painful exercise. Nevertheless, seeing dysfunction for what it is will allow team members to shed their denial and do away with rationalizations. Furthermore, as team members open up to what is wrong, they will look for answers regarding how they can do things right. In this sense, you as a leader have a unique opportunity to redefine responsibilities while clarifying and assigning critical roles. This is what Jeffrey Lurie, Frank Esposito, and David Helfer were all able to do. They identified harsh realities and brought them into public view, taking this critical first step toward turning their teams around. By acknowledging the problems, the people on their teams were able to move forward, strive toward loftier goals, and put their focus back on winning and working together.

This first stage is a cold shower of truth. It feels good only after it's over, and once it's done, the organization is revitalized and energized to move forward. With dysfunction out in the open, the real work can begin.

2

Stage II: Committing to Growth

In stage II, your team is poised to move forward, and it's time for the team's focus to shift from what's wrong to what's possible. Team members are fed up with losing. They recognize that change is needed and are committed to growth. Your team has gone through the emotional exercise of confronting its inadequacies and acknowledging them, but it now needs direction. It wants to progress and leave the losing ways behind, but it may not know where to go or how to get there. It needs something to believe in as it pushes out of the haze of failure, and it will look to you for guidance. The team at stage II needs a vision for where it's going, clear values to guide it, and a decisive plan of action that's chock-full of specific and attainable goals.

At stage II, there is a lot of enthusiasm about what lies ahead, but teams at this stage are also quite fragile because they lack the confidence that comes with years of success. This is a stage for the dreamers, the planners, and the believers, and you can push the group forward quickly with a passionate and credible aspiration for the future.

As we explore stage II, we will look at three organizations and the leaders who gave them the vision, values, and goals they needed. Bill Polian, the architect behind one of the biggest turnarounds in the history of the National Football League, is among the most aggressive visionaries in professional sports. In his ability to dream big and inspire others, he is second to few, and his insights into what a vision could and should be are invaluable. Similarly, Jim Grundberg and his business partner, Jason Pouliot, brought life to a lifeless brand, the SeeMore Putter Company, which, as the company's name implies, designs and manufactures golf putters. In reviving that promising organization, they set out to establish clear values they would live by, work by, and grow by. Needless to say, SeeMore Putters is still following that early code but is now considered one of the hottest properties in the putter industry. Finally, Jere Harris, co–lead producer of *Spider-Man: Turn Off the Dark*, has one of the most compelling turnaround stories going. Harris buckled down and worked with his colleagues to establish a clear plan and accompanying goals, and he is now atop Broadway with a successful show. All three of these leaders took their organizations from stage II to heights previously unimagined, and yet each one started with the belief that things could in fact turn around. Stage II is about defining the future because great achievements can't occur without the hope of making them happen.

LAUNCH THE VISION

For a team to move from catastrophe to conquest, the group has to define a path forward. As teams rise up, they have to develop and embrace a vision for the future. What's possible? What are the hopes? What's next? What are the dreams? A vision is intended to provide direction, motivation, and clarity. The vision focuses effort and inspires action by defining where the group is going. A vision is intended to capture possibility and may seem incredibly unrealistic to a team numbed by failure. Nevertheless, in spite of how ridiculous a vision may seem, it's the responsibility of the leader to articulate and sell it.

As far as visions go, few in professional sports have proved better than Bill Polian at selling grandiose dreams under incredibly unrealistic conditions. Polian walked into the Indianapolis Colts at a time when it was one of the worst franchises in the history of the NFL. He established a vision for winning the Super Bowl, and then he got to work, leading one of the most dramatic transformations in professional football. In fact, the Colts have to be in the running for advancing one of the most preposterous visions of any professional franchise in the history of American pro sports. When Polian walked into a moribund

Indianapolis franchise after the 1997 season, he unequivocally stated that his vision for the team was "world championships." At the time he proposed this vision, the Colts were arguably one of the worst franchises in the National Football League. But more than ten years and one Super Bowl championship later, Polian's conviction for his early vision is still very much apparent. As he says, he "made no bones about it. Didn't apologize for it. Didn't care whether people thought it was possible or not. That was our goal—we wanted to win the world championship."

When Polian dedicated the franchise to Super Bowl victory, the Indianapolis Colts had a reputation for losing. Since 1978, when the NFL inaugurated its sixteen-game season, the Colts had never won more than ten of their sixteen games, whereas various NFL teams had reached that milestone 172 different times over the same twenty-year period. The Colts' average annual record from 1989 through 1998 was 6 wins and 10 losses, and the 1991 team has been immortalized as one of the worst in NFL history, establishing a franchise record with 1 win and 15 losses. It's a struggle to identify with a loser, and in those years, as TV cameras swept through the Hoosier Dome during home games, Colts fans wore paper bags over their heads to avoid the embarrassment of being seen wasting their time and hard-earned money supporting the dismal franchise.

As further evidence of how absurd Polian's initial vision seemed, the Colts' futility in Indianapolis also had a long pre-history. Originally based in Baltimore, the franchise had become a joke even before the move west. The Baltimore squad, defined regularly by its foibles and failures, racked up a total of 2 wins and 25 losses over the 1981 and 1982 seasons (a strike shortened the 1982 season to nine games). As a result, the 1981 and 1982 Colts are considered two of the worst teams in the history of pro football, and in 1983 the dreadful Colts fell short of .500 yet again, ranking at the bottom of the eastern division of the American Football Conference (AFC). To add drama to debacle, the Colts franchise, to avoid being seized by the city of Baltimore in a political power play, literally sneaked away to Indianapolis under cover of darkness in the early morning hours of March 29, 1984. Football fans in Indianapolis were initially ecstatic about the unexpected arrival of a new pro football team, and season-ticket sales spiked to unprecedented levels. But the honeymoon quickly ended as the newly relocated Colts amassed a 12-36 win-loss record over their first three seasons in Indianapolis. And even this dismal showing was only a small sampling of things to come.

In addition to the Colts' on-field failings, the franchise's front office struggled with the team's general management. Few top draft picks came to Indianapolis, and those who did were quickly traded, or they played out their contracts and left. Not only were players in and out, between 1989 and 1998 the organization went through five head coaches. Indianapolis finished the 1997 campaign at the bottom of the AFC, with a 3-13 win-loss record. The franchise had made the playoffs only once in the previous ten years, and there was little reason to see any light on the horizon. It was at this point—what seemed to be rock bottom—that owner Robert Irsay made a critical play and convinced Bill Polian to come in as president and general manager and try to stop the bleeding.

Polian had already proved himself a winner, but this was a big project. Before heading to Indianapolis, he had built a reputation for being something of a turnaround specialist as general manager of the Buffalo Bills, a team he had taken, in eight years, from back-to-back 2-14 seasons to three consecutive Super Bowl appearances. Similarly, when Polian took his skills to the Carolina Panthers, he quickly created a winner—the Panthers competed in the championship game of the National Football Conference (NFC) when the franchise was only in its second year. Clearly, Polian had shown himself capable of reversing the fortunes of bad and unproved franchises, but could he work his magic on the Colts? Not only had the Colts been struggling on the field and in the front office, they had relocated (under historically sketchy circumstances) to a midwestern city without a demonstrated fan base. There were a lot of concerns surrounding the Colts, and it seemed highly unlikely that they'd be winning a Super Bowl anytime soon. Simply setting their sights on the playoffs alone would have been a formidable vision.

A vision has to be unique to the organization and must assert a sense of purpose while also being practical, if not wholly attainable.[1] Needless to say, when Polian walked into the Colts organization and announced that the Indianapolis Colts were going to become a championship-winning franchise, people scratched their heads. Polian, reminiscing about those initial days, says, "When you come into one of these jobs where there hasn't been a long history of success, and you're as committed to it—some might say messianic—as I am, they think you've got a screw loose, and it will never happen." So for Polian and the Indianapolis Colts, it wasn't enough that he stepped in and encouraged the organization to go after a world championship. He also had to ground the vision, proving to the front office and the on-field team that it was attainable, and that they could do it. He had to communicate the vision and sell it, and he knew it wasn't going to be an easy job.

Selling the franchise on a hopeful future took not only the science of advancing a vision, but also the artistry of conveying it. The manner in which a vision is communicated can make or break a team's eventual success. A vision that is articulated as a substanceless cliché certainly won't help the cause, and may actually damage it. In addition, a vision that fails to inspire visible and communicable action is easily abandoned.[2] Moreover, if a leader isn't capable of following through with a vision, or if the leader doesn't "walk the talk" by communicating what he or she aspires to through what he or she does, then the vision will simply be ignored.

To take this idea one step further, here are some detailed recommendations that can assist leaders in their efforts to clearly communicate and inspire others with a vision:

1. *Be concrete.* The actual words used to articulate and communicate a vision have an impact. The more concrete and straightforward the language, the easier it is for people to

buy in. Concrete statements that team members can digest and unequivocally understand are more apt to incite forward movement and eventual progress.[3]

2. *Ask for input.* It may seem counterintuitive, but messages are heard more clearly when they are part of a two-way dialogue. A powerful way to gain a group's approval is to ask for input regarding how the group can change and where it can set its sights.[4] Although a leader is in no way obligated to act on every opinion he or she hears, going through this process can uncover valuable information and perspectives that might not have been considered initially. When opinions and ideas are solicited, followers are likely to feel that they have a voice and own a small part of the eventual vision.

3. *Communicate consistently.* Something as simple as consistently communicating the efforts needed for change is a key predictor of eventual success.[5] It's not simply about the act of forming the statement, unveiling it, and trusting that everyone gets it. Along the way, a leader needs to continually communicate how his or her actions are connected to the larger vision. In short, consistent and repeated action is necessary for a vision to take hold, and how a leader links his or her actions to the vision can effectively move things along.

4. *Communicate effectively.* Effective communication of a vision can actually have an impact on the perceptions that team members have of their leaders. In fact, the manner in which a vision is communicated affects how team

members see their superiors.[6] Imagine that! As a leader strives to turn an organization around, the language and the crafting of a vision may actually influence others to see that leader as both more effective and charismatic.

In spite of all the how-to tips, the truth is that the advancement of a vision is not an exact science. It's not an "If you do this, then your vision will impact your team" proposition. It requires patience, persistence, and the wherewithal to know that there aren't any magic bullets. The vision simply represents an effort to convince the team that change is possible—to motivate team members to strive for something more than the lackluster reality of the present day. It's a tool that, if implemented persistently and patiently, can inspire the group to keep toiling toward a shared end.

What is perhaps most compelling about Polian's efforts to turn the Colts around is just how committed he was to communicating his vision in such a difficult and muddy situation, and how much sacrifice was ultimately needed. Critical decisions had to be made, and each decision sent a specific message about how the team would need to change to attain the new vision.

Polian recalls one such decision. "We had decided that we would release the incumbent quarterback, Jim Harbaugh, who was quite popular with some segment of the fans. We didn't think, since we were going to draft a quarterback, that it was good to have a veteran in the wings sort of looking over his shoulder." It was a tough sacrifice for the fans as well as for the team, and it was a difficult choice for a general manager who had been on the job for a matter of days, but it was necessary for the growth of the organization. Working to clearly communicate where the franchise was headed, Polian called Harbaugh into his office and gave him the news as simply and honestly as possible. He recalls saying, "Look, you tell me where you would like to go. If there is no particular place where you'd like to go, we'll release you. Whatever you'd like to do, we will do, but you're not in our plans going forward, and I don't want to create the illusion that you are."

It was a difficult step and a difficult conversation, but it's this type of straight-up, decisive communication that made this newly formed vision clear to the entire franchise. Regarding this particular decision, Polian concludes, "It sent a message to everyone else in the building that this was the new way of doing things." The message couldn't have been any more apparent—the Colts were working toward winning the Super Bowl.

Following that decision, Peyton Manning was drafted as the face of the changing franchise, $9 million was committed to a facility that gave the players a new weight room and a new locker room, and the players were fed breakfast and eventually lunch. Polian asserts, "It sent a message that we're part of the new, modern NFL, and we're investing in facilities that will help you be better players." In time, the Colts slowly morphed into a team that was hungry to win, eventually fighting for playoff victories and for Super Bowl rings.

All the while, commitment to and communication of the vision never stalled. Polian remembers one detail from late in a back-and-forth game with the Baltimore Ravens that took place at the end of the 1998 season. During a botched play in the fourth quarter, some miscommunication occurred between Manning, then the rookie quarterback, and Marvin Harrison, his wide receiver. If they had communicated correctly, Polian explains, they probably would have won the game. Later, in the locker room, Polian approached the two players and said, "Listen, I don't want you to give a second thought to what occurred out there today. This off-season, you will work together so much that this will become second nature. The next time you see that defense, it's a hookup and a touchdown pass. I know it's gonna happen. I've seen it happen with Jim Kelly and Andre Reed, and it will happen with you." Polian was committed to tirelessly communicating a clear message— the Colts were going to be winners.

Polian was relieved of his position with the Colts in January of 2012, after a disastrous 2011 campaign in which the Colts managed only 2 wins, but his legacy as one of the greatest turnaround artists in the history of professional sports remains intact. Although 2011 was marred by a season-ending injury to Peyton Manning, as well as by other personnel issues, Polian accepted blame, noting that he had made mistakes. Nevertheless, throughout his tenure with the Colts, Polian's efforts largely paid off, as shown in Figure 2.1. The 1998 season, Polian's first with the Colts, ended with only 3 wins and 13 losses, but in the twelve seasons that followed, the Colts amassed 125 wins and 51 losses, for a winning percentage of .710. More impressively, the Colts advanced to the playoffs

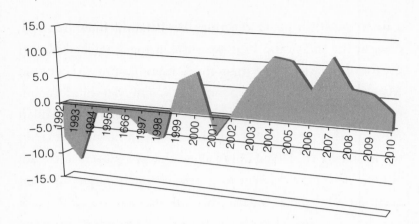

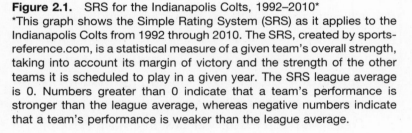

Figure 2.1. SRS for the Indianapolis Colts, 1992–2010*
*This graph shows the Simple Rating System (SRS) as it applies to the Indianapolis Colts from 1992 through 2010. The SRS, created by sports-reference.com, is a statistical measure of a given team's overall strength, taking into account its margin of victory and the strength of the other teams it is scheduled to play in a given year. The SRS league average is 0. Numbers greater than 0 indicate that a team's performance is stronger than the league average, whereas negative numbers indicate that a team's performance is weaker than the league average.

eleven times, and in 2005 they won the Super Bowl. For Polian, constant communication of the larger vision, emphasis on the small efforts to achieve the larger dream, and clear and decisive language and actions were all part of this early turn-around phase.

In stage II of the turnaround process, leaders need to inspire and guide. Polian's vision for the Colts was clear, and his efforts didn't waver. He was convinced that the franchise could win a Super Bowl, and he communicated that conviction explicitly, with words and actions. As Polian defined this path at stage II, his vision gave the Colts a focus that eventually spun them around, guiding them from failure to unprecedented levels of success.

ADOPT GUIDING VALUES

In addition to articulating a clear and inspiring vision, leaders guiding teams through stage II need to answer questions about how advancements will be made. At this stage of the process, guiding values provide needed structure for how the group will work to move forward. People are stirred by values, and they want to invest in organizations that share their ideals.[7] As the leader, your determining team values and making them explicit motivates those around you. You have to make it clear that the group stands for something, whether it's customer service, effort, innovation, or something else entirely. When you do that, the shared commitment will motivate specific actions by providing a framework for what's important, what's expected, and what's needed to see that the larger vision is achieved.

In September 2006, when Jim Grundberg and Jason Pouliot purchased SeeMore Putters, the company had essentially flatlined, with no sales or distribution. As they prepared for the relaunch of SeeMore Putters, the duo had a clear vision of creating "the greatest brand in golf" but needed clear values to guide the way. Building up to the launch, they identified just how they wanted SeeMore Putters to become a premier brand. Grundberg explains, "If we provide great customer service, a technology that we already know is validated, and create some new and exciting product designs, we felt like this thing could end up being a great brand." In other words, the vision wasn't enough to get them where they wanted to go; they also had to define just how they would try to get there. Grundberg and Pouliot placed emphasis on getting behind the exciting and unknown technology at SeeMore Putters, but, more important, they also dedicated themselves to providing great customer service and creating innovative designs. They set their values around customer care and cutting-edge product development, and with these guiding principles they began their lifesaving operation on an all-but-lifeless brand.

Seven years earlier, SeeMore Putters could have become a brand on the rise. Payne Stewart had just won the U.S. Open with one of the most spectacular putting performances in the history of the event—and did it with a SeeMore putter in hand. The brand instantly gained international visibility. Sadly, however, four months after winning the U.S. Open, Stewart died in a plane crash on October 25, 1999, and golf lost the player many considered one of the kindest and best-hearted of all time. The golfing community mourned—and SeeMore Putters faded from view. As Grundberg notes, "With the tragic accident, losing Payne at the end of 1999, the brand sort of disappeared off the radar screen. It kind of came and went really quickly." The brand was then sold to some investors who had limited visibility and involvement in golf, and SeeMore Putters was effectively shelved.

SeeMore Putters was a brand that had never had much of a life, but when Grundberg and Pouliot stepped in, it was a good match from the start. Not only did SeeMore Putters offer a unique product that the partners believed they could leverage, Grundberg and Pouliot also had previous experience on a team that had taken another brand in the same industry from nearly nothing to something. Earlier in their careers, they had been colleagues at Odyssey, a brand focused on the design and development of golf putters. The team at Odyssey grew the brand, then unknown, to a number-one market share, creating one of the biggest success stories in the history of the putter industry. With that experience, and with SeeMore Putters' unique history and technology, Grundberg and Pouliot were confident about their chances.

Because Grundberg and Pouliot had put such intense focus on the two distinct values of customer service and technology, they wanted to attract new customers as well as customers who had experience with SeeMore Putters. To accomplish this goal, they offered new and inventive products along with unparalleled accessibility and a fervent focus on customer care. Their attention to these values can be seen throughout the organization, and it touches everything from product delivery to customer relations. For example, SeeMore Putters makes putters available on a wholesale basis as well as through direct sales, bucking the more traditional sales model of choosing either one channel or the other. Some would scoff at this model as a recipe for sales suicide, arguing that this strategy alienates wholesalers with the threat of competition from direct sales. But Grundberg argues that ensuring availability and accessibility is good customer service. "We're not going to limit you through various channels," he explains. Some customers prefer to buy from a pro shop, and others are comfortable buying online. SeeMore Putters offers customers as many options as possible.

This commitment to customer service extends far beyond purchasing convenience. In a world dominated by voice recordings and phone trees, SeeMore Putters is dedicated to being different by being accessible and accommodating. As Grundberg explains, "That's been the number one part of our whole value chain—customer attention. A meeting will never interfere with taking a call from customers or taking an e-mail, and it's almost a 24/7 immediate response." It's a commitment to serving the people interested in the product and willing to invest in the brand. Grundberg makes this clear when he says, "If you need a putting lesson on a Saturday afternoon over the phone, give us a call. We'll give it to you." For Grundberg and company, to spend a Saturday giving a putting lesson to a customer is worth the time. Giving back to the people committed to the brand is not simply good advertising. It's what the people at SeeMore Putters value.

In addition to customer service, SeeMore Putters is equally committed to the development and innovation of putter technology. In 2010, *Bloomberg Businessweek* described the small company's $1.5 million in sales as a function of an inventive and diverse product line that caters to both high-end needs and to more modest ones.[8] And even though SeeMore Putters has diversified, with innovative products that serve a variety of needs, the company is adamant about not innovating for innovation's sake. Grundberg notes, "It's important to keep up with good technologies from a marketing perspective, but when you start changing technologies just for the sake of change, we jump from authentic product development to just a world of consumer marketing." In other words, SeeMore Putters values technological advancement and product development, but not at the expense of customers' expectations and needs. The focus is on innovating where innovation is needed, on creating a genuine benefit for the customer, and on developing new technologies that serve a functional purpose.

At SeeMore Putters, this commitment to the specific values of customer service and innovative technology has paid continual dividends. In the two years (2005–2006) before Grundberg and Pouliot acquired the company, SeeMore Putters had less than $50,000 in total revenue and sold its products in five countries. Between 2007 and 2011, the company experienced at least 30 percent annual growth, brought in $8 million in total revenue, and shipped its putters to more than forty countries.

Along the way, Grundberg and Pouliot and their team have managed to stay true to themselves. Although the SeeMore team is small—only about ten people—the team's values are intact. Given this type of focus, it's no wonder that SeeMore Putters is experiencing success. With the vision of creating "the greatest brand in golf," SeeMore Putters set the bar high, but with a strong commitment to clear values, Grundberg and

Pouliot and their colleagues are making headway as a recognizable, reliable, likable brand.

ESTABLISH A PLAN AND SET GOALS

If your vision and values are a bridge taking you to a new frontier, your larger plan and smaller goals are the bridge's girders and rivets. Goals hold the plan together, providing team members with guiding objectives and clear, measurable milestones. As with every other aspect of stage II, teams are looking for direction and craving a clear path forward. The vision provides the team with a direction, and values determine the manner in which the team will advance, but a plan with goals serves as the road map that guides the team to its destination, one stop at a time.

Some argue that making a strategic plan has become passé.[9] Others say that strategic planning is a useless exercise that a team rarely follows through on.[10] Yet few would make the argument that plans do not help to focus the direction of a team. Larger plans can keep people motivated when smaller goals aren't achieved.[11] They also enhance the likelihood that goals will eventually be attained.[12] Through plans and corresponding goals, teams and organizations are able to visualize a path forward while maintaining the focus needed to advance to the finish line.

Jere Harris, a successful businessman, is chairman and CEO of PRG, an industry-leading company that supplies production equipment to live events worldwide. He is also the lesser-known and less public co–lead producer of the musical *Spider-Man: Turn Off the Dark*. Michael Cohl, the show's other co–lead producer, is a legendary concert promoter and producer whose reach in the music industry has extended from Michael Jackson and Frank Sinatra to the Rolling Stones and U2. In 2009, when Harris and Cohl came aboard the *Spider-Man* project, it was badly failing (see Table 2.1). The media were circling the production like vultures, making it the focus of scathing criticism while fueling the belief that the show would never move from development to production. But in June 2011, because of a savvy plan and a laserlike focus on the specific goals required to make the production successful, Harris and Cohl effectively launched the show on Broadway.

When they were brought aboard as co–lead producers in 2009, it was imperative that Harris and Cohl immediately establish a plan for getting the stalled *Spider-Man* musical moving. Harris's company had been providing support for the technical aspects of the production, and Cohl had been working as a behind-the-scenes producer, and so both men had experience that helped them understand what would ultimately need to be done. But neither of them had been as involved in the production as they would eventually become.

In 2005, the show's original producer, Tony Adams, had suffered a terminal stroke in his office while signing U2's Bono and the Edge to write the show's music. Adams's business partner, David Garfinkel, then took the production reins and

Table 2.1. Chronology of *Spider-Man*'s Turnaround

Year	Month/Day	Event
2003		Tony Adams, original producer, asks U2's Bono and the Edge to write the show's songs.
2005		Adams suffers a stroke and dies. His business partner, David Garfinkle, takes over as producer.
2009		Garfinkle exhausts the original $25 million budget. Bono asks Jere Harris and Michael Cohl to take over as co–lead producers.
2010		
	March	Key actress Evan Rachel Wood drops out of *Spider-Man*.
	April	Key actor Alan Cumming drops out of *Spider-Man*.
	November 14	The first preview performance is delayed two weeks, to November 28.
	November 28	The preview finally occurs. The first act is stopped five times and ends prematurely with the Spider-Man character stuck dangling above the audience.
2011		
	February 7	*New York Times* theater reviewer Ben Brantley calls the production a "national joke"; *New York Post* theater blogger Elisabeth Vincentelli calls *Spider-Man* "an inconsistent, maddening show that's equal parts exciting and atrocious."
	February 9	*New York Post* theater reviewer Michael Riedel predicts that *Spider-Man* will close by September 2011.

Table 2.1. (Continued)

Year	Month/Day	Event
	March 9	Director Julie Taymor steps away from day-to-day production; Philip William McKinley takes over.
	April 17	Previews are suspended, and the production goes on a brief hiatus.
	May 12	New previews begin.
	June 14	The refurbished production's opening night takes place.
	June 15	Patrick Healy, writing for the New York Times, notes that the production "unfolded flawlessly" before an audience that included Bill Clinton, Bono, the Edge, and Julie Taymor, the show's "director of record."
	September 14	Contrary to the predictions of the New York Post's Michael Riedel, not only is Spider-Man still around, the show welcomes its 500,000th patron.
	November 29	Spider-Man sets the weekend box-office record for the Foxwoods Theater, pulling in more than $2 million over the Thanksgiving holiday.

moved the project along for a couple of years until he hit an impasse in the form of repeated delays in the renovation of the theater he had chosen for the production. Eventually Garfinkel ran out of money and had difficulty raising more to keep the project alive.[13]

By 2009, the *Spider-Man* project was essentially stuck. Through the later months of that year, as the project stagnated, the creative team, including not just Bono and the Edge but also visionary director and co-writer Julie Taymor, became restless. Garfinkel still couldn't get the funds to keep the project moving, and Bono, the Edge, and Taymor had too many industry connections to sit around and wait.

As Harris tells the story, the production "was on its last breath" when Bono called him at home and invited him and Michael Cohl to a meeting. Harris and Cohl accepted the invitation, met with Bono and company, and heard about the current state of the production. Harris and Cohl were ultimately asked to be more involved, and they left the meeting to think about whether they'd become co–lead producers. The situation was dire, but Harris and Cohl were both successful CEOs of prominent entertainment companies, and they both knew a winning pitch when they heard one. Taking a hot international property like *Spider-Man* and putting it together with some of entertainment's most creative and successful personalities made sense to them. They believed in the *Spider-Man* concept, even though it needed a lot of work. After a brief deliberation, Cohl and Harris partnered in their commitment to seeing the show move forward, and they accepted the invitation to become the show's co–lead producers.

Once they officially came on board, in late 2009, Harris and Cohl concocted a plan for what would have to happen. Harris says of this early period, "We decided that we thought we could rescue it—that we could fix it." But, he admits, they knew "it would be a monumental task."

Their plan contained two distinct objectives that would serve to guide all energy and action in the months ahead. One, they had to raise money and, as Harris says, "financially restructure the whole business end." Two, they had to "get the production back on track and get it running in the theater." Both were formidable tasks. Even before it opened, the show was already getting horrible press. In addition, Evan Rachel Wood and Alan Cumming, the actors slated to play two key roles, both dropped out of *Spider-Man* in early 2010. Raising more money wasn't going to be easy. And if coming up with tens of millions of dollars to reignite the business end of the production was one thing, it was quite another to reinvest in the cast and crew in a way that would raise confidence and inspire a hit musical. To tackle both issues together seemed nearly impossible.

Nevertheless, by November 2010, about a year after Cohl and Harris stepped in, the show was ready for previews. Taymor, along with Bono and the Edge, had creatively set out to break new ground with an innovative and revolutionary production, and with Harris and Cohl supporting them, the project seemed feasible, if a stretch. But the budget ballooned beyond expectation as Taymor and her creative team pushed the technical and conceptual boundaries of Broadway.

The first preview performance, after several postponements, finally took place on November 28 and received terrible reviews. Patrick Healy of the *New York Times* wrote, "The show stopped five times, mostly to fix technical problems, and Act I ended prematurely, with Spider-Man stuck dangling 10 feet above audience members."[14] Audiences were confused by a convoluted and cluttered story line, and the heartbeat of the production was dull and hard to find. To add to the drama, five actors had been injured on the set throughout the course of rehearsals and preview performances.[15]

Blood was in the water, and the critics were frenzied. One review after another lambasted the production, proclaiming its inevitable doom. Although Broadway preview performances are generally practice runs with live audiences and are intended to hammer out last-minute issues, those early *Spider-Man* performances became occasions for critical self-analysis. Harris and Cohl had concerns, to say the least.

Harris had expected the show to develop during previews, but that wasn't happening. "Even though the show was performing," he explains, "we weren't rehearsing and making large changes."

But more than $30 million had been pumped into the initial plan of getting the business and the production back on track, and with this level of investment, Harris and Cohl weren't going to let the show suffer. With the initial plan complete, they recalibrated their sights and developed a new plan to create a great show. To see this new plan through, they had to go step by step through a short list of three specific, interrelated, challenging goals: to understand what the audience wanted, to keep the cast and crew on point, and then to relaunch a new and improved product. For most Broadway productions, this would have seemed like a critical moment, one when the entire show would have been brought into question. But Cohl and Harris were unfazed, and they moved forward one goal at a time.

According to Edwin Locke and Gary Latham, experts in business management, goals impact performance in four ways: they direct attention, they energize, they increase persistence, and they drive action.[16] Locke and Latham also note that "high (hard) goals lead to a higher level of task performance than do easy goals or vague, abstract goals."[17] This point is integral to the story of *Spider-Man*'s turnaround because, like it or not, there was nothing easy about the goals that Harris and Cohl needed to achieve.

"The success or failure of Broadway shows after opening night is really up to the audience," Harris explains. He and Cohl had come to terms with the fact that the critics hated the show, but more important than the critics was the fact that audiences weren't raving. Harris and Cohl wanted to know why, and they needed to figure it out. If they were going to deliver the experience they were aiming for, then they had to know more about what the audience wanted, what worked, what didn't, and what should be there that wasn't. And like the good businessmen they were, they sought feedback.

"We're scientific," Harris says. "We're math guys, Cohl and I, and we did what any guy who had $50 million invested would do. We went to our customers and did focus groups."

The feedback was clear. The audience had trouble following some story elements, such as a mythlike reinterpretation of the original comic book-based story of Spider-Man. But

Julie Taymor and her creative team disagreed with this feedback from the audience.

"We had a great team," Harris says, "but if the team doesn't jell, it doesn't work—you don't win. So we had a team that wasn't jelling."

In order for a team to achieve its goals, every one of its members needs to agree to work toward the same thing. But Taymor and her team were standing by their creative product while Harris and Cohl were calling for change. This impasse compromised the entire production, and the outcome was unfortunate.

With little delay, Taymor and her colleagues were relieved of their roles, the show was shut down, a new preview schedule was announced, and a creative team dedicated to meeting audience expectations was put in place. Philip William McKinley was brought in to direct, Roberto Aguirre-Sacasa assisted with the story, and Chase Brock helped with choreography. (In spite of their differences with Taymor and her team, Harris and Cohl have honored their efforts by keeping their names on the show's website.)

"I think we found the right folks," Harris says, "and we were able to shut the show down for roughly three and a half weeks. We opened the show up right on schedule, did our thirty previews, and opened the show as we said we were going to do."

The team jelled. Difficult changes were made, a tight schedule was kept, deadlines were met, and the new team delivered what Harris calls "a big hit show."

But such massive change in such a short time warrants fear, and anxiety was high. McKinley, the new director, spent time with the young lead performers to keep them calm and confident. The rest of the cast and the crew rehearsed with a newfound discipline. As for Harris and Cohl, they came up with an additional $15 million to carry the production to its intended reopening.

Opening night for the refurbished production was June 14, 2011. Harris says of that evening, "We had fought back, and here we were. For us it was the end of a long, long, long journey. It was rewarding, it was difficult, but we survived and succeeded."

Simply reopening the show, in spite of all the obstacles, setbacks, and criticisms, would have been success enough, but the production is up and running smoothly. From the June 2011 reopening of the show to the following December, *Spider-Man* grossed between $1 and $1.7 million per week, consistently leading all Broadway productions.[18]

Given everything that happened, it's no wonder that Harris points to the first night of the second set of previews, and to the official reopening night, as the two highlights of his time with *Spider-Man: Turn Off the Dark*. Both nights brought redemption, proof that sticking to a plan and hitting key goals can pay off. It was tough along the way. There was a lot of slogging and a lot of sweat, but Harris and Cohl and their team made it to the finish line, and Harris himself will forever look back on both evenings as critical achievements in a long and drawn-out battle.

Yes, *Spider-Man* struggled, and the press has told that story. But the story that's not being told is the one about inspiring persistence and shrewd planning, about never giving up, about digging deeper when the chips are down, and about having the guts to implement a plan and goals that may not be easy but are necessary for survival and success.

THE PLAYBOOK FOR COMMITTING TO GROWTH

Stage II is an opportunity to define where your team is going to go and how it's going to get there. It is about the future. For your team members to see what the future can be, you must create a vision that will appeal to them. This is what Bill Polian did when he stepped into the ramshackle Indianapolis Colts franchise and announced that the Colts would be competing for Super Bowl championships.

It is your right to make bold claims for your team's future. Such visions may seem downright crazy, but they can also begin to inspire a team to reach heights previously unimagined.

How the vision is going to be achieved is just as important as the vision itself. The framework for the vision is established with values, and as an organization slowly begins turning around, you must establish unmistakable values for how things will be done and for where the focus will lie, just as Jim Grundberg and Jason Pouliot did with SeeMore Putters.

Finally, you need to develop a plan and goals to direct your team through the growth process and toward eventual success. A clear plan is a map for how a team will eventually achieve success, and the goals are the smaller steps throughout the process. This is what Jere Harris, co–lead producer of *Spider-Man: Turn Off the Dark*, did as he worked alongside his colleagues to create a plan and goals that eventually transformed the production from a stalled concept into a thriving Broadway show.

Stage II is about understanding and committing to the need for change. Team members have to move past the mediocrity they've embraced in the past. Teams at this stage are in need of savvy leaders who will help determine not only where to go but also how to get there. In stage II, you will draw a blueprint for your team's future success.

3

Stage III: Changing Behaviors

S tage III is a time when you will define, model, and reinforce the behaviors that are right for your organization's growth. Because every organization is different, it is critical that you focus on the behaviors that are appropriate for your team. There's no guidebook for what those behaviors are, but your vision, values, and goals can help direct the way. Stage III is a stage of action, and it represents a distinct shift from planning to doing. At this point, you will begin to see your plans through. The problems have been identified and embraced, a road map for the future has been developed, and now is the time to focus on the daily efforts needed to move the team forward.

Throughout stage III, behaviors will be scrutinized, praised, and modeled. What's right for your team may not be right for others. A unique outline for how to act as a champion needs to be developed, and the focus on doing should be constant. Stage III is composed of small and consistent efforts that will steadily move your team forward, but the constant plodding can be tiring, and there may be times when advances seem to be of little consequence. This can feel frustrating and disorienting, but even when you're forced to question whether or not you're on the right path, keep moving forward. Stage III is not about big wins but rather about the small successes of gradual growth. Your continual efforts to teach, model, and reinforce what's right will pay cumulative dividends as they start to add up.

This stage is tedious at times, but it is an early stage of development, and behaviors for future success are being defined. Your team members will learn how to carry themselves as winners, and you're responsible for showing the way. Leaders in stage III have to focus on providing their teams with insights into how and what they need to change while also providing the motivation to do it. All eyes will be on you as the leader, and your ability to actively teach team members about how they can change for the better is essential. Equally important is your ability to model what success looks like while also establishing winning guidelines. Throughout this stage, behaviors will change for the good as previous, losing habits are broken and even the smallest of successes are celebrated as evidence of progress.

Ani Shabazian, Marilyn Masaitis, and Kim Mulkey are three leaders who have effectively turned their organizations around by modeling winning ways while shaping the behaviors of their teams. All three of these leaders turned failing organizations into thriving entities in little time and have profoundly impacted the groups they have led. Although they share minimal common ground in their backgrounds and professions, their ability to change the behaviors of struggling teams with confidence, compassion, and consistency is noteworthy. Ani Shabazian took over the Loyola Marymount University Children's Center (LMUCC) at a critical moment of failure, but she was driven to change the defining behaviors of the team. Marilyn Masaitis bought a failing diner on a heartfelt hunch, and she modeled how to be a success. Finally, Kim Mulkey, head coach of Baylor University's women's basketball team, has made a Hall of Fame career out of molding her players and teams into winners. All three leaders have masterfully guided their organizations through stage III, changing the attitudes and behaviors of their teams en route to profound and oftentimes unexpected achievements.

TEACH BEHAVIOR

In stage III, change is afoot, but as the team sets out in this newly defined direction, the old ways must be left behind. Ani Shabazian took over the Loyola Marymount University Children's Center when it was in profound disarray. The center had degraded to the point where child safety was in question, and turning it around was a formidable task. Shabazian was dedicated to teaching her team the behaviors needed for success. It was a tough sell, but Shabazian believed that with time and persistence, the group could provide world-class child care services to the Loyola Marymount University (LMU) community.

In 2006, the behaviors of the staff at LMUCC were woefully suspect. Cathy McGrath, a mother of two and a professor at LMU, had entrusted the center with the care of her children, and she says of those days, "It would just be a mess." There were complaints and concerns regarding sanitation, the education and interests of employees, and the general care of the children enrolled. When McGrath walked in one day to find her youngest daughter, an infant, swaddled tightly in a blanket and lying on her stomach for naptime, she reacted. "I just sort of grabbed her," she recalls. "It was such a visceral moment. I just picked up my daughter and ran out of the center and was just, like, 'Oh, I don't know if I can bring her back there.'" It's dangerous for newborns to sleep on their stomachs, and they can suffocate when swaddled tightly and left lying facedown. McGrath was right to be concerned, and at the time, she arranged for her babysitter to take on more hours.

During those days, concerns were warranted. Enrollment was down, the relationship between the facility director and parents was caustic, and programs were canceled. It wasn't that the teachers and administrators were intentionally neglectful or abusive—make no mistake, it was a caring and affectionate team—but it was as if they didn't wholly understand the toll of their mistakes, as if they didn't know better. One child had contracted Methicillin-resistant Staphylococcus aureus (MRSA), a highly contagious and difficult-to-treat staph infection, outside LMUCC. McGrath recalls watching a teacher who "changed one child's diaper, put that child down, picked up another one, and put him right back on the changing table without changing the paper, without wiping it down with a cleaning fluid like they're supposed to. And this was right during the time when they were having the outbreak of staph." It was clear that the need for change was vital.

McGrath's story is reflective of a widespread loss of trust between parents and the LMUCC leadership and staff. This led to a minor restructuring that had a major impact. Responsibility for LMUCC was moved from Finance to Human Resources (HR), and Rebecca Chandler, vice president of HR, and Heather Alexander, director of Benefits, headed up the early change effort. Initially they set out to find what was broken, and they proceeded to fix it. First they gathered up data in an attempt to diagnose the problem. They conducted a comprehensive satisfaction survey and held open forums to hear employees' concerns. As Rebecca remembers, "That data really set our charge for us because there was high dissatisfaction, there was high turnover, there was low morale, there was a lack or a huge deficit in staff engagement, and so we knew that our charge was to try to turn this unit around." Rebecca and Heather truly believed that the center could be better, and so they established a vision for turning it around, identified key goals and values, and then started to act. They began with a search for a new director, and eventually they scored with the hiring of Ani Shabazian.

Landing Ani was a big win for LMUCC. In spite of her initial refusal, Rebecca and Heather persisted until she came aboard. With a Ph.D. in child development and five years of experience running the Infant Development Center at the University of California, Los Angeles (UCLA), Ani brought instant credibility. She had received her master's degree in education from Harvard, and while at UCLA she had been awarded the Distinguished Faculty Teaching Award, an honor recognizing the most skilled "masters of the classroom" on the basis of letters from colleagues, students, and former students, in addition to course evaluations. Ani also had the temperament for the job. She was warm, she was passionate about child development, and she was confident enough to overcome early concerns.

When Ani arrived, the situation was a mess, and she admits to having felt overwhelmed, but she had committed to changing the center and refused to back down. She initially relied on education. She set out to ensure that all the teachers at the center actually had the necessary education to perform their jobs. Astonishingly, they didn't, and as Ani worked to implement this initial change, certain teachers immediately lost interest in staying at the center. Some didn't want to pursue further education, but for those who did, Ani acquired funds from the university to pay their expenses. She recalls that the teachers who didn't want to stay "naturally sort of left because they knew that they'd have to put in more time and more effort in order to still maintain the same job that they had six months prior." In short order, the team was changing, and Ani was doing everything she could to make sure that the changes would stick for good.

Education comes in many different forms, and multiple efforts to communicate information are more likely to stick than one singular effort.[1] With this in mind, Ani was committed to educating her staff in multiple ways. Although she insisted on a minimum educational level, she also worked to personally convey information to her staff members in order to ensure that they would avoid falling back into poor habits. Remember McGrath's story about children's diapers being changed on a table that had not been adequately sanitized? Ani says, "We started with health and safety. We got them bleach bottles. . . . I trained them on how to do the bleach, and I trained them on health and safety practices, how to use gloves when someone is bleeding." These personal efforts also included pointing out unacceptable behaviors. In one instance, Ani walked into a classroom and noticed a teacher listening to an iPod. She confronted the teacher, explaining that it was inappropriate to be in a classroom with an iPod on. By pointing out specific examples of behaviors that were no longer acceptable, and by working with staff members to help them adopt new behaviors, Ani was continually promoting change.

While Ani was focused on helping the group members understand what they needed to be doing on a day-to-day basis, Rebecca and Heather were educating the staff members about how they contributed to the larger university. "They needed education and awareness of how they fit—the contribution that they make, and how important what they do is to the university," says Rebecca. She and Heather were encouraging the staff to change as individuals, and once again Rebecca recalls that it required "talking, listening, meetings, lots of meetings, bringing in other people from other areas so they could explain to them what they did." Behavior change is best supported through multiple efforts and channels, and staff members at LMUCC were being supported through formal and informal education led by Ani as well as through the reassurance of Rebecca and Heather.

Beyond the benefit of multiple education methods, behavior changes within teams are best supported by environments where people feel safe to make mistakes and are supported by their leaders.[2,3] In addition to the efforts Ani was making to educate her staff, she needed to foster a safe environment where ideas could be shared and mistakes could be made. When she arrived at LMUCC, the climate had been the opposite of safe. "It was interesting," she recalls, "because when I first started, I felt that everyone was scared to death—or not necessarily scared, but everyone had their guard up, and I'm pretty approachable." Ani went straight to work, breaking down barriers and taking the time to invite the ideas and perspectives of those around her. "I did a lot of observations," she said. "I had one-on-ones with all the staff members. I met with them, I talked with them." Ani developed trust by making herself accessible. In the process, the staff began to know and understand her.

While the one-on-ones were helping to build rapport, Ani worked to create safety in other ways as well. Just weeks into her new position, an irate parent came into Ani's office, screaming. In a measured and neutral voice, Ani said, "Let's have this conversation when you're a little more calm." Not only was the frenzied parent shocked by Ani's unruffled response, a nearby staff member also expressed surprise. Ani was curious about her staff member's reaction, and later she asked her about it. The staff member replied, "The former director would have yelled back." Ani's efforts were in stark contrast to those of the center's previous administration. More important, the calm manner in which she handled conflict helped to foster a supportive environment, one that encouraged the behavior-change efforts she needed her employees to embrace.

Through these efforts, the ball started moving. The behaviors of the group slowly started to change. Rebecca recalls, "The staff was now being held accountable in ways they were not accustomed to." Parents were taking notice of the professional demeanor of the teachers, and the teachers became more heavily invested in the changes that were taking place. Enrollment began to rise, and the children's center was soon getting attention for its achievements.

Cathy McGrath, the once apprehensive parent, tells a story that illustrates the drastic behavior changes that occurred among LMUCC staff members. One morning her husband dropped off their youngest daughter, Jane, who was between two and three years old at the time. He noticed his daughter back away, as if scared, from a seemingly aggressive child who was eager to play. McGrath's husband immediately voiced his concern to the teacher that his daughter might be getting bullied. The teacher listened, and over the course of the day she took three or four pictures of that child and Jane playing together. She e-mailed the pictures to McGrath's husband, explaining, "I thought about what you said, and it's a really valid concern, and wanted to let you know that this is how they interact during the day. Also, to address your concern, we've decided to seat them next to each other at lunchtime so that they can pass the food and the bowls to each other so that they can have another way of interacting that's collaborative and cooperative." McGrath was amazed at the immediate response.

The center slowly progressed from being an organization in crisis to delivering a reliable service to eventually becoming highly respected in the industry. When she arrived at the center, Ani held the seemingly far-fetched goal of the center's becoming accredited, and by 2010, LMUCC had joined an elite 8 percent of child care centers nationwide by receiving full accreditation. In 2011, Ani and the children's center were still growing, but all the smaller efforts had begun to add up. She still had challenges, although the challenges she is facing today have changed. She explains that enrollment numbers are now through the roof, and she jokingly laments, "My poor administrators are being harassed constantly with 'Where am I on the wait list?' and 'Why can't I get in?' We only have 105 spots, and there's 1,600 people on campus. I can't accommodate them all." Clearly, the problems are drastically different from what they once were.

Ani hopes to one day transform the children's center into a lab school, where children and families can be monitored and assessed through the university as a means to further the discipline of child development. Changes continue to occur, but it seems that the more things change, the more changes Ani has planned. As Ani says, "We still have so much room for growth. We're constantly growing, and I think that's a strength. When you think that you've stopped growing is when stagnation sets in."

For LMUCC and Ani, growth is the theme, and progress is a continual effort. The turnaround has been dramatic, but in the early phases the focus on behavior change was critical. Through formal and informal education, through the reassurance of organizational leaders, and through Ani's persistent encouragement of positive change, early goals were achieved. Throughout stage III, Ani and LMUCC were simply focused on adopting the right behaviors.

MODEL BEHAVIOR

Beyond educating team members about how and what to change, you must exemplify the change you want to see in your team. Stage III is all about action, and your own actions are incredibly important, not simply for what they accomplish but also as a way of communicating information related to the values and climate you're working to establish in your organization.[4]

Sometimes an organization has a crucial figure whose actions and efforts set a tone so strong that it not only guides the organization but becomes a part of it.[5] Such an organization is guided by a leader who defines what a winning team looks like, and who does that by serving as an example for the larger group. At Marilyn's Cafe, in Chester, New Jersey, that person is the cafe's owner, Marilyn Masaitis.

Marilyn currently inspires her staff with her consistent attention to detail and her concern for customers and employees, but her role was once very different. Before owning Marilyn's Cafe, Marilyn worked on-site, waitressing for nearly twenty years to make ends meet as a single mother of two. The actual diner that is now Marilyn's Cafe has been through seven different owners, and it dates back to 1968, but Marilyn's early involvement spanned only two owners and two decades.

Early in her career, Marilyn had waitressed for George, a genuine friend who had managed the restaurant successfully, even though his efforts might have been at the expense of his employees. Marilyn worked for George for nearly eighteen years before asking for a raise from her $2 hourly wage. When George refused to increase her pay, Marilyn left. Business immediately started to suffer. George called Marilyn, asked her to come back, offered her a raise, and made it clear that he was gearing up to sell the business. Marilyn agreed to come back for a new hourly rate, and with the understanding that she would leave once George sold the business.

Two years later, Cesar bought the place from George, but after eighteen months business had not taken off. The cafe was bombing. It needed to be sold, but there were no buyers. Eventually Marilyn was approached because of her emotional ties to the restaurant and her positive reputation with the local clientele. Marilyn deliberated. She had worked her entire life and didn't have much money to spend, but when the price dropped by $50,000, Marilyn took the deal. She was nervous, but she had overcome challenges before, and she had reason to be confident. She had worked for $2 an hour for eighteen years, had gone through a divorce, and had been a young single parent of two boys. She knew the value of hard work and genuineness, and she knew the profound nature of trusting relationships (eventually she married someone she connected with, trusted, and loved). She believed that if she just focused on being herself, things could work out, and she was gutsy enough to put her hopes into action.

Marilyn made her mark immediately. She changed the sign out front to read MARILYN'S CAFE, and she ran a single advertisement in the local newspaper, simply announcing "Marilyn's Back." Under Cesar, the décor had been stark and impersonal, with generic posters of fruit and vegetables. Under Marilyn, the décor is important, and it shows all over her cafe's walls. She has collected Harley-Davidson gear and pictures of Marilyn Monroe and Elvis, and she has put up encouraging signs that say things like NEVER, NEVER GIVE UP and her favorite, WE MAY NOT HAVE IT ALL TOGETHER, BUT TOGETHER WE HAVE IT ALL. She welcomes the gifts of customers and friends, and she displays items that have been brought back from other countries or that were once lost in basements or attics. "Most of the Marilyn Monroe things people bring from vacations," she explains, and she highlights the signed and numbered plate a customer brought back in his briefcase from Bangkok as well as the gold bust that another patron had stored in her basement for forty years.

Marilyn takes great pride not just in how the cafe is decorated but also in how clean it's kept. She says, "When I get twenty or thirty women walking out of the bathroom, and even men walking out of the men's room, who go, 'It's so nice to go to the bathroom in a clean bathroom—I can't imagine what your kitchen looks like,' I say, 'Go back and look.'" In fact, she's had some folks take her up on the offer, and she's happy to oblige. Marilyn strives to run a transparent and close-knit shop. She treats her customers more like family, inviting them into her world of cleanliness, nostalgia, and inspiration, and even letting them into her kitchen.

All of this helps create an environment that is clean, safe, and comfortable, but in addition to how she maintains her restaurant, she goes to great lengths to foster commitment among her team members. Her cook is a carryover from Cesar's reign, and when Marilyn took over, he was in his early twenties. There was no reason to believe that he could help Marilyn succeed, because his cooking obviously hadn't been drawing in big crowds under Cesar, but Marilyn saw a spark in the young cook. When the place changed over to Marilyn's Cafe, the cook asked to stay. Marilyn bluntly asked why she should keep him, and he said, "I'll try my hardest." She believed him, and she saw him as an honest guy who'd become stuck in a failing restaurant. She asked him what he'd made under Cesar, and he told her $400 per week. She told him she would raise it to $500, and that he would start the next week. He was obviously surprised, but she explained that the raise was intended to motivate him and focus him on working hard so that he could learn how to excel. He's been with her every day since then, he never misses work, and Marilyn brags about how he makes the best soups in the world. Marilyn took a risk by challenging a young, unproven cook to get better, and now she has a loyal employee.

Marilyn cares dearly for all her staff members. As someone who has waitressed nearly her entire professional life, she knows that if the restaurant is making money, the staff is making money. She talks with the waitresses about how important it is to smile, about how they shouldn't focus on their own problems when talking to each other and the customers, and about how they should work as a team (for example, filling up an empty coffee cup even when it's in someone else's section, or getting the cook a drink when it's busy, and so on). After all, the restaurant is open 365 days a year, and Marilyn herself is there every day, working and helping out with a smile.

She has high expectations, and she talks openly of a great guy she let go for not showing up. It wasn't personal, but, as she says, "I'm big on dedication. I was dedicated to this place for twenty years, for somebody else. You don't let people down." By firing this employee, she made it clear to everyone else that she demands performance—and, on the flip side, that if you meet her demands, she takes care of you. If a waitress or another staff member is going on vacation, she'll hand that person some extra cash to go out and enjoy a meal or two. If she hears a waitress talking about something she saw in a store but couldn't afford, Marilyn will go buy it and give it to the waitress for Christmas. A few years ago, she gave her cook a hand-painted guitar for the holidays because he loves music and couldn't afford one. She remembers what it was like to raise kids and wait tables, and she enjoys helping her employees. More important, these actions show her employees that she truly cares about her team.

Marilyn goes to great lengths to reward and mentor her employees, but it's also worth highlighting how she behaves in critical moments, during crises. The day-to-day actions and behaviors of a leader drive an organization forward while also defining the manner in which it's moving. In a crisis situation, however, the actions of a leader can leave followers with a powerful and unforgettable imprint, either good or bad, that can have a lasting impact on the organization, sometimes for years. In essence, the manner in which a leader responds to a crisis can influence the very culture of an organization.[6]

In the restaurant business, crises come in all shapes and sizes. For example, take the unexpected power outages that can occur after a thunderstorm sweeps through Marilyn's small

New Jersey town. Power is critical for most businesses, but it's essential for a restaurant. If you can't cook, you can't make money. Add to that the large quantities of perishable foods that may be spoiling in the quickly warming refrigerator, and it can make for a pretty bad day. Rather than fret about issues she has no control over, Marilyn simply uses the gas burner to boil water for coffee, and business sails along as usual. She credits her customers, saying that they think it's "no big deal" and actually enjoy the break from the regular routine. Customers may not be able to cook at home, but power outages at Marilyn's Cafe are warm events where they can talk and wait out the storm.

Beyond rainstorms and power outages, Marilyn also weathers the natural storms that come with relationships. She works hard to build relationships with her customers, and she is genuinely concerned if such a relationship becomes compromised. She tells the story of a couple who regularly came in on the weekends but then abruptly stopped. She doesn't take the absence of a regular customer lightly, and so she sought the husband out at his workplace and inquired about what had gone wrong. He explained that he had had a bad experience—cold, hard toast. Marilyn asked him for another shot, and then she went to the apartment of the waitress who had served him. The girl was scared, but Marilyn gently explained, "Those customers that come in every Saturday and Sunday and leave you a $5 tip—that's $10 in the course of a weekend, and this is what you did to them." The girl understood, and Marilyn concluded, "You don't serve people what you wouldn't eat yourself." Needless to say, the couple came back, appreciative of Marilyn's efforts and concerns.

Marilyn's commitment to relationships doesn't stop with her customers. She also fights for her employees. She has a profound sense of fairness, and she reflects on an exchange she had with a customer who was making derogatory comments about the work ethic of immigrants in general. Marilyn employs several immigrants, and she politely told the customer, "No offense, but don't insult my people. They're on the up and up, they're good guys, and they work very hard." Whether a crisis comes in the form of a power outage, a missing customer, or an insult to her employees, Marilyn follows her heart and is willing to take chances. When confronted with a crisis, she is willing to stick her neck out, and it shows in the success of her restaurant.

Marilyn's actions are essential for developing a climate in which her team can be successful. She constantly demonstrates that she values her restaurant, her customers, her staff, and the blue-collar ethic that has guided her through the years. Her actions provide a guidepost for her team. Team members at Marilyn's Cafe don't have to guess at what Marilyn thinks is important. They know just by watching her. Marilyn consistently does what she thinks is right, and her behaviors serve as powerful examples of where her employees' focus needs to lie, but they also remind her customers that what they see with Marilyn is what they get. Through her actions, Marilyn reminds customers and employees that they are valued, and they repay Marilyn with their loyalty.

REINFORCE BEHAVIOR

Throughout stage III, your team is actively changing. Some team members will leave, and others will adopt the behaviors necessary for the group to advance and move forward. It is essential that the leader model the desired behaviors for the developing team while also educating team members about how and what they can change. Nevertheless, a keen leader also reinforces the needed behaviors through celebration and critical feedback. Kim Mulkey, head women's basketball coach at Baylor University, in Texas, has become something of an expert on how to reinforce the behaviors of teams aspiring to win.

By the time Mulkey took the job of head women's basketball coach at Baylor, in 2000, she had already accomplished more than most people will in a lifetime. As a player, Mulkey had led her Louisiana high school basketball team to four straight state championship titles, and she followed that up with four Final Four appearances and two NCAA national titles for Louisiana Tech. She crowned her accomplishments with gold medals at the 1983 Pan Am games and the 1984 Olympics. As a coach, she assisted her collegiate alma mater for fifteen years, coaching in seven Final Fours. To put it simply, in her long athletic career Mulkey had never been associated with a losing program.

But when she accepted the job at Baylor, she embarked on a new journey. She left her home state, she left Louisiana Tech, and she left winning behind. She was taking over a program that played in the NCAA's Big 12 Conference, a reputable conference for all sports, but the women's basketball team had very little history of success. For the 1999–2000 season, the season before Mulkey arrived, the team had gone 7-21 and at one point was riding an 11-game losing streak. Add to that the fact that it was Mulkey's first time as a head coach, and it's no wonder that she looks back and says, in her slow Louisiana drawl, "Initially I cried for the first two to three months after accepting the job, because I was just not sure if I'd made the right move." But Mulkey's a fighter, and she quickly dried her tears, pushed the fears aside, and went to work, relying heavily on her past successes as a player and a coach. She soon hired a staff, one that she knew would stick around for a while, and then hit the recruiting trail to fill out her roster.

As Mulkey got to work, she needed to instill the intensity, work ethic, and discipline that had been embraced by her past championship teams. For these new behaviors to stick, however, the players had to understand what needed to be done, they had to be able to do it, and they had to have the appropriate reinforcement. Mulkey drew on her experience and guided the team in the way that she knew best. "You must discipline players for anything that you deem inappropriate in representing your school and your program," she explains. "You're not going to be thrown under the bus for a mistake. To me, a mistake is not a mistake until you make it twice." She was forgiving and understanding but also firm and disciplined.

Mulkey drew a line, and the players were expected to meet her standards.

Over the years, Mulkey has had to hold firmly to her expectations. She's very clear that discipline and consistent effort are essential to being a player on her teams, and she's not to be tested. She remembers when a starting player was falling below team standards off the court. Her disappointment is still obvious as she recalls, "I dismissed a starting player in the middle of the season for continuing to skip, miss classes. I believe that there's a point where you draw a line in the sand and say 'Okay, no more.'" Her action sent a clear message to the player as well as a resounding message to the rest of the team. The remaining players had a clear example to draw from—skip class, leave the team. There were no questions about what would happen if a player, even a starter, cut class, and the known consequence was a sufficient deterrent. Mulkey says, "You know, a lot of coaches wouldn't do that, particularly if they're a starter," and she's right. In the effort to ensure that a program is as competitive as possible in the short term, many a coach would allow such a player to keep playing, but that also sends a clear message to the team—it's okay to miss class, and the coach doesn't really mean what she says, especially if you can help her win.

Mulkey is quick to point out that the way a punishment is doled out is important, and that the intent behind the punishment is meaningful: "I think if a player sees that you are for them, that the demands you make on them are not to break them or tear them down but to make them a better player, then they will do it for you." She realizes that her intentions need to be transparent, and that punishment isn't an end in itself but a method for helping the player and the team improve.

Although Mulkey has had to dole out punishment at times, she has also handed out her fair share of encouragement and positive reinforcement. "You make sure you mix in some laughs and some hugs," she says, "and you let them know that there's a time to work and there's a time to play." Recognizing that her methods have changed in the twelve years she's been on the job, Mulkey recalls, "Back then, I could get on the floor and demonstrate drills, taking charges, high-fiving those kids, getting on them in a way where you just say, 'No, that's not good enough. You can do better.'" By getting on the floor, she reinforced what she wanted out of her players and how they should be playing the game, and she did it while also providing a clear visual model. She was encouraging them with high-fives and showing them that she was willing to get in there and do the hard work.

Along with these on-court efforts, she was deliberate in celebrating successes. She remembers her first year at Baylor, when the squad wanted to win more games than the seven it had won the previous year. When the players won their eighth game, they had a celebration. Similarly, after the victory that assured a winning season, they had another celebration. They also celebrated when they beat their first opponent that was ranked in the national polls. Celebrating each milestone provided the team with further proof that the behaviors that had

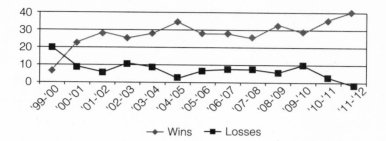

Figure 3.1. Wins, Losses, and Postseason Achievement for Baylor University Women's Basketball Team, 1999–2011*
*In addition to the wins and losses shown in this graph, the Baylor women's basketball team amassed the following record of postseason achievement: 2000–2001, NCAA first round; 2001–2002, NCAA second round; 2002–2003, Women's National Invitation Tournament (WNIT) runner-up; 2003–2004, NCAA Sweet Sixteen; 2004–2005, NCAA champion; 2005–2006, NCAA Sweet Sixteen; 2006–2007, NCAA second round; 2007–2008, NCAA second round; 2008–2009, NCAA Sweet Sixteen; 2009–2010, NCAA Final Four; 2010–2011, NCAA Elite Eight.

taken them to that point were actually working, that the group was on the right track, and that if the players continued they would experience similar results.

As Figure 3.1 shows, Mulkey's team has come a long way since she took over in 2000. The Baylor Bears have been to nine NCAA tournaments. They've had five Sweet Sixteen appearances, two Final Fours, and in the 2004–2005 season they went home with the national championship. Amid all that success, one memory that Mulkey points to involves, appropriately, a celebration toward the end of that first season. ESPN, the sports network, had chosen the Lady Bears as one of the teams to be filmed live during the network's NCAA tournament-selection broadcast. Mulkey looks back: "I remember the very first NCAA tournament [selection] after the first year, and how we gathered at a place and watched it on television." She remembers because her team was "part of the biggest turnaround in college basketball." The team that had won a meager seven games the previous year, against questionable competition, was selected to play in its first NCAA tournament. That achievement, which had seemed far beyond the team's reach only a year before, was an indication of the incredible things to come.

Kim Mulkey taught her team members how to play like champions by supporting them, motivating them, and reinforcing her expectations with consequences and celebrations. When players fell below the standards, Mulkey relied on strict discipline. When the players elevated themselves, Mulkey celebrated and patted them on the back. Mulkey was clear, and the consequences were consistent. There wasn't much gray, and the players followed the guidelines. In the process, effort was increased, attention to detail was scrutinized, and performance was elevated. By establishing clear guidelines that would shape the practices and habits of the team, Mulkey turned a perennial loser into a champion.

THE PLAYBOOK FOR CHANGING BEHAVIORS

Stage III is the time for action. It is the time to educate your team on how and what to change, to model the behaviors needed for future success, and to establish clear guidelines that are celebrated when they're met and critically examined when they're not. Stage III is still early in the process of a team turnaround, but it's indicative of progress. You will need to put in continual effort, but even when it seems hopeless, you will need to stick with it. If you look for teachable moments, as Ani Shabazian did, model desired behaviors, as Marilyn Masaitis did, and celebrate the smallest of successes, as Kim Mulkey did, your forward movement will be clear and tangible. Winning starts with small and regular behaviors. The big wins won't come easy, but stage III is characterized by the small and consistent behaviors that will eventually add up to bigger successes. Progress may seem slow, but no matter what happens, keep moving forward. Even when you have to wipe away the tears, focus on the positive gains, and keep advancing.

4

Stage IV: Embracing Adversity

By now you're nearly halfway through a long and most likely arduous effort, but the big wins are starting to come. Stage IV represents a swing in attention away from daily behaviors and on to the obstacles that lie in front of you. In stage IV, challenges are not only accepted but also embraced as a means to show your stuff. Setbacks and obstacles should be welcomed because you're excited to prove that you're better than you once were. These challenges are a means to test your mettle, build resilience, and get even stronger. This is an exhilarating stage, where confidence is beginning to beam and the proof that change is occurring is in the team's efforts to accept and overcome new challenges.

Almost all teams will momentarily battle the temptation to revert to the older and oftentimes easier ways of mediocrity. It's easier not to care, try, or risk losing. When you're determined to move forward, however, challenges are opportunities to test yourself—guideposts for continual growth. As you advance through stage IV, your ability to interpret challenges as opportunities, while persisting resiliently through obstacles, will be imperative.

Two organizations notable for their grace and efforts in working through stage IV are Domino's Pizza and the Los Angeles Angels of Anaheim, a Major League Baseball (MLB) team. Both organizations accepted and welcomed the challenges that typify stage IV, but for different reasons. Domino's and its executive team saw the obstacle of poor customer satisfaction as an opportunity. The company embraced challenges as a means to further redefine itself as it set out to establish new standards for success. In a similar spirit, Bill Stoneman, former general manager of the Angels, saw opportunities in the franchise where others saw setbacks. He used those opportunities to develop a degree of resilience in the club that eventually led the team to a World Series win. Both organizations exemplified the essence of stage IV through their confident willingness to take on adversity in their efforts to improve.

TURN CHALLENGES INTO GROWTH OPPORTUNITIES

Leaders and organizations that perceive obstacles and change as an opportunity continue to advance by becoming stronger. In contrast, organizations that see similar situations as threats become overly focused on preservation.[1,2] One turtles up, shielding itself from the threat of change, whereas the other pushes forward, eager to embrace the new. Oddly, these distinctions are simply perceptual. They represent thoughts that can actually be controlled, and at this stage of the turnaround process, organizations are capable of perceiving the more positive option.

Domino's is an organization that has made the most of the challenges it has had to face, choosing to perceive crises as paths to new success. According to Yvon Chouinard, cult business hero and founder and owner of Patagonia, "When there is no crisis, the wise leader or CEO will invent one. Not by crying wolf but by challenging the employees with change."[3] This sentiment may seem disruptive and counterintuitive, but for Domino's communications vice president Tim McIntyre and his colleagues on the executive team, it has proved amazingly successful.

The National Restaurant Association, the industry's leading association and advocate, releases a monthly restaurant performance index (RPI). The RPI is indicative of the health of the industry, and it measures the industry against a steady-state number of 100. If the RPI for a particular month is 100, then there is neither growth nor contraction in the industry. Any number above 100 indicates positive growth, and any number below 100 indicates contraction. In 2008, the restaurant industry was hurting, and not in a small way. In December of that year, the RPI came in at 96.4, indicating not only a record low but also the industry's fourteenth straight month of contraction. Similarly, the Current Situation Index, a measure that examines trends in the industry on the basis of four key indicators, was then at 95.7, also the lowest level ever.[4] For Domino's, this measure indicated a 4.9 percent contraction in U.S. in-store sales.[5]

As if the larger problems experienced by the restaurant industry weren't enough, Domino's executives were also noticing issues more specific to the company's place in the market. McIntyre, who has been with Domino's for more than twenty-five years, explains, "For forty-eight years we were essentially known for promoting delivery. We were known for convenience and value." Domino's had built an empire on the promise of delivering pizza whenever and wherever you needed one, and it kept itself on the top of the market for a long time by doing just that. At first, Domino's delivered when no one else would, and then, when more restaurants offered delivery, Domino's answered with a thirty-minute guarantee. Over time the marketplace changed, and the uniqueness of delivery started to slide. Domino's had put all its eggs in one basket— the service side of its business. But, as Russell Weiner, chief marketing officer, explains, "Chinese food started to deliver, and forget about food. Amazon came to life, and Netflix gives you movies that are delivered immediately. So, suddenly, if all you want to hang your hat on is delivery, you've got to really up your game." For Weiner and the Domino's team, delivery was no longer a novelty that could support the business.

At the end of 2008, Domino's could have simply shrugged and blamed its sliding sales on the larger economy and the Great Recession that had impacted every major player in the industry. But with these devastating realities crashing down on the company, the executive team chose to do the opposite. They saw the current hardships as an opportunity to force change, to reinvigorate the organization, and to generate positive momentum. They advanced a crisis by questioning their core product—their pizza. In its fifty years, Domino's had never touched its pizza recipe, but with the focus on delivery no longer novel, and with the larger restaurant business suffering, they didn't see any other choice.

Domino's pizza was the logical target for improvement for two obvious reasons—it was the company's central product, and consumers didn't like it. Patrick Doyle, Domino's CEO, is recognized for being transparent, up-front, and honest with his customers, colleagues, and partners. He doesn't shy away from the truth, and he says that 2008 "was pretty lousy for us. Our old pizza did better when our brand was not associated with it. When we put it in a Domino's Pizza box, [consumers] thought less of the quality of the pizza. That's a pretty darn big problem. We had negative brand equity around pizza quality." As difficult as it was to accept, the Domino's Pizza brand had become synonymous with poor quality. The company image had become so tarnished that people were more apt to like the product if they didn't know it was from Domino's.

Domino's used the downturn in the economy and competition in the delivery space to ask, "Who can we be?" In order to help answer that question, the company actually embraced the negative feedback from customers in what is now considered revolutionary terms. First, in 2008, Domino's internally set out to build a new pizza, one that would stand up to competitors in a blind taste test. As McIntyre recalls, "They tried dozens of doughs, dozens of sauces, dozens of cheeses, to try to find the ones that people liked. That took two years, and all of this was internally hush-hush and very top secret." The company dedicated itself, in obsessive fashion, to the development of a new recipe. The team was determined to deliver a good pizza.

As Domino's secretly worked to change its pizza recipe, the company also launched a line of sandwiches. The sandwiches were sold to franchises with the promise of wooing lunchtime buyers while also diversifying the company's product line. In a sense, the sandwiches bought some time, pushing sales and traffic up while boosting the company's credibility with franchise owners. By the end of 2009, Domino's was the only national chain with positive same-store sales, which compare sales in a given month to sales during the same month of the previous year.

While franchise owners were buying into the organization's new direction, Domino's at the corporate level was focused on the pizza rollout. Building up to the launch of the new product, Domino's publicly proclaimed that the company agreed with consumers that Domino's pizza was inferior. This decision was a radical step, on a number of levels. In the first place, invoking the downside of the product and actually going on record to say that the pizza wasn't good enough proved to be a marketing first. What was less obvious is that by openly admitting that the company wasn't happy with the current recipe, Domino's avoided any temptation to back out or make a quick escape. The brass at Domino's clarifies this tactic by saying that it was like destroying escape routes in a military battle. As Doyle, McIntyre, and Weiner all explain, they created a dynamic whereby they couldn't retreat and surrender wasn't an option.

It seems brash and maybe shortsighted, but this self-imposed effort to eliminate all escape motivated the team to push that much harder. In December 2009, Domino's aired *Domino's Pizza Turnaround* on YouTube, launching the new pizza while reflecting on and sympathizing with the ardently critical comments about the old pizza. The video was honest and open, and it explained why Domino's had made the change and where the company was planning to go. It also launched a renewed corporate image, one that the organization and its customers have wildly embraced.

Once the new pizza went to market, Domino's ran the numbers and organized focus groups, and the company watched its earnings rise as the positive feedback poured in. As Figure 4.1 shows, in the first quarter of 2010 (the first quarter for measurements since the new pizza hit

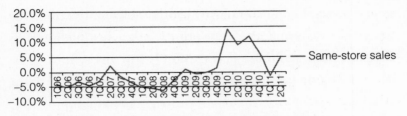

Figure 4.1. Same-Store Quarterly Sales, Domino's Pizza

the streets), same-store sales were up 14.3 percent, an increase that was possibly the largest same-store sales jump in any quick-service restaurant chain in a decade. The uptick was proof that the company's efforts were paying dividends, and the leadership at Domino's didn't look back. Domino's sales were up 10 percent in 2010, and Weiner, talking about the results, says, "For our industry, let alone our brand, up 10 percent is kind of unheard of." Domino's was obviously pleased with the numbers, but, more important, the company's efforts to accept setbacks and embrace challenges had forced tremendous growth.

Domino's dealt with the challenge openly and honestly and received high marks from the public, but this wasn't the chain's first rodeo. In April 2009, while the organization was in the midst of secretly developing the new pizza recipe, two franchise employees in a small North Carolina town had filmed themselves contaminating sandwiches and then posted the clip to YouTube. The video had quickly gained steam, and news stories began popping up all over the Internet. Patrick Doyle cut his vacation short and flew back to the company's headquarters in Ann Arbor, Michigan, to address the issue with his executive team. The clip was pulled, Domino's assured customers that the food pictured in the video had never been delivered to customers, and the two employees were fired and criminally charged.

The incident was dealt with, but that wasn't enough. The company was still obliged to contend with the public relations fallout. In a revolutionary marketing move, Domino's seized on the Wild West landscape of social media and immediately took action. Doyle and McIntyre jotted down key talking points, grabbed a video camera, and headed down to the lobby to film a message for their customers. Doyle sat on a stool and spoke candidly and passionately to the camera. He intended to assure customers that although an unsavory incident had occurred, it had been dealt with. As McIntyre remembers, "We just wanted to say, 'We found it, it's a hoax, and thanks for sticking with us.'" Their video was posted on YouTube in such a way that it could be retrieved with the same search terms as those used for the original stunt video.

What had started as a PR nightmare became a national story about Domino's clever use of social media and about the company's notable commitment to honesty, customer satisfaction, and humility. According to McIntyre, "By the time *USA Today*, the *New York Times*, CNN, and ABC got wind of the story, it was no longer about two people tainting food at Domino's, which is what it could have been. The story was, 'How do companies protect themselves in the YouTube era?'" By handling the issue quickly and cleverly, the company turned a potentially devastating story into a positive tale about Domino's cutting-edge efforts.

For Domino's, embracing challenges has become a defining shift. That shift has proved to be a welcome change among consumers, and it's also setting a bar for how companies will deal with difficulties in the future. As Domino's turned itself around, the company used its own vulnerability to become stronger. As McIntyre affirms, by embracing the realization that the pizza had to change, the executives "also realized we were setting a standard here for honesty and transparency." Their approach is both refreshing and inspiring because it speaks to the opportunity that all challenges can present.

This renewed focus has put Domino's in a position where the company can question its processes and make changes fluidly. More recently, Domino's has gone so far as to move on an internal decision to no longer use heavily styled food photography or dress up its ads with unrealistic images of the company's products. As the company confronted the ethical concerns it had about doctored photos of food, Domino's even invited customers to send in photos of Domino's pizzas, whether those pizzas were good or bad. The effort was coined the "Show Us Your Pizza" campaign, and it has proved to be yet another game-changing public relations and marketing move. The vast majority of submissions are of good pizzas, but when photos of bad ones come in, the company addresses them. Doyle says, "We showed a pizza that was stuck to the box and was a mess. I went on television and apologized for it, and consumers loved it. They loved the fact that we were saying that sometimes it doesn't look the way it should. We do mess up, and we apologize for that, and if we do, let us know and we'll fix it." For Domino's, mistakes are now opportunities to communicate openly with customers and the public. While Domino's obviously works to minimize mistakes, when mistakes inevitably happen, they're welcomed and dealt with.

By creating challenges and embracing unanticipated setbacks, Domino's has adopted a way of perceiving problems that has led to the continual refinement of the company's product, processes, and messaging. The Domino's team is confident, believing that it is capable of triumphing over whatever issues may crop up. It welcomes challenges, even creating some from time to time in an effort to help the company grow stronger. By seeing the opportunities in impediments and problems, Domino's uses its trials and tribulations as a means to advance. Setbacks and obstacles are nothing more than tools that push the organization to become better. They are seen as necessary for growth, and as the natural pangs of development. Where Domino's is headed is anyone's guess, but the company's revolutionary marketing and management tactics are in the books and are the direct result of embracing challenges as opportunities.

BUILD RESILIENCE

Challenges are opportunities for those skilled in identifying and capitalizing on them. When properly taken advantage of, these moments can grow an organization and make it stronger. In addition to looking at challenges with an open and eager mind, those who are resilient to the debilitating potential of upheaval and impediments are likely to advance. Seeing challenges as opportunities is an important component of stage IV, but equally important to effectively turning your team around is the ability to take difficulties in stride and bounce back from things that are damaging. Resilience is essential. Fortunately, it can be developed and enhanced.

Resilience is best described as a mix of emotional skills. It is found at the intersection of a variety of abilities and attitudes—being optimistic, being self-confident, being socially connected, being flexible—that guide an individual through adversity and stressful situations.[6] Bill Stoneman, former general manager (GM) of the Los Angeles Angels of Anaheim, is a poster boy for these qualities and drew on his resilient attitude to turn his team around.

Stoneman saw opportunity in the Angels that many had overlooked. He saw hope for success where others had seen the futility of a franchise in an unsupportive market. In spite of what others thought, Stoneman was undaunted by the challenges that came with turning a weak franchise into an MLB power, and he never wavered in his optimism that the Angels could be a contender. But before the Angels could soar, Stoneman had to find a way to teach his new ball club about the power of resilience, and about why it was a key ingredient of success.

Today—in a time that will prove historic for Major League Baseball, but for all the wrong reasons—Stoneman seems like a character from the glory days. History will look back on Major League Baseball at the turn of the most recent century for its steroid scandals and big-money dominance, but Stoneman found success with principles that hark back to pro baseball's initial turn of the century. In a nod to the bygone years of Connie Mack and Edward G. Barrow, Stoneman plodded at his own pace, built a successful franchise on a foundation of people of good character who weren't afraid to work for success, and did it with a rugged sense of resilience, staying positive while moving forward one decision at a time.

Stoneman was born in Chicago in 1944 to a mother who was a longtime Cubs fan and a father who was a fervent fan of education. As a pitcher for the University of Idaho's baseball team, the younger Stoneman had the NCAA's lowest earned-run average for 1966. He went on to get a graduate degree at the University of Oklahoma and then had a modest pro career. In the late 1960s and early 1970s, he played for three pro clubs over the course of eight seasons, pitching two no-hitters during his tenure as a notably hardworking slinger. But at 5 feet, 10 inches, and at 170 pounds, he was undersized as a pitcher and eventually hung up the spikes when he shredded his shoulder hurling heat. After his time in the pros, he spent a number of years away from the game, working at a Canadian financial company, but he was inevitably wooed back when the

Montreal Expos offered him an opportunity in their front office. Stoneman worked in the Expos' front office for sixteen years and then landed the GM gig with the Angels and never looked back. He jumped in with both feet, and in 1999 he began one of the quieter yet more memorable GM careers of the modern game.

Although Stoneman had been hired in 1999, it wasn't until 2002 that his dreams came true. As a point of reference, in the ten years leading up to Stoneman's arrival, the Angels had compiled a 738-817 win-loss record, winning only 47.5 percent of their games over the course of a decade. In 2002 and the four subsequent years, the squad finished with a 452-358 record—a 55.8 winning percentage. In that somewhat magical turnaround year of 2002, the Angels won the American League Championship Series (ALCS), the American League Divisional Series (ALDS), and the World Series. Stoneman clearly had turned the franchise around, but what's noteworthy is how he did it, and the attitude he did it with.

Optimism and positivity are key ingredients of resilience. Positive thinking allows an individual to perceive a situation as a challenge rather than a problem.[7] When Stoneman first stepped into his role as GM, he walked into a culture that focused on problems and accepted mediocrity. "They accepted that they were a midmarket club," he says, "and you heard that a lot. The bar was set low." More than anything, for Stoneman the acceptance of mediocrity represented a loss of hope, a pervasive negativity that didn't make sense. After all, Los Angeles was a city with money. Individuals and families could afford to come to games, and there was a myriad of local companies that could afford box seats and sponsorship packages. The challenge, he explains, was that the Angels "just hadn't bought into it." In more clichéd terms, Stoneman saw a silver lining in what most saw as a dark cloud, and he went after it.

Stoneman believed that the club could be a consistent title contender, and he wanted a field manager who shared not only his belief but also his resilient mind-set and willingness to stick with the job until it was done. He decided on Mike Scioscia, who was considered a risky selection at the time. Scioscia had played in the majors for fifteen years, but he had minimal managerial experience, having guided the Los Angeles Dodgers' AAA (minor league) team for only one year, with mediocre results. Some may have scoffed at Stoneman's decision, but he explains that he wanted "a guy with some energy," one who would "command the respect of the players," and that Scioscia had the "toughness" and "dedication" necessary for the job. For Stoneman, previous achievements are not always that important when compared to the promise an individual brings to the table—his character, his grit, his fighting spirit. "What's a guy's ceiling?" he asks. "What's he going to be? It's not about where someone is right now." Stoneman and Scioscia put together a crew of coaches who were full of energy and credibility—guys they knew to be passionate, dedicated, and knowledgeable. They hired guys they wanted to work with, but, more important, they hired guys they believed would hang in there during the difficult transition, guys who would continue to inspire and guide a team of young players in spite of the inevitable struggles.

The idea of developing a resilient team didn't stop with the coaches: "We did have to change the mind-set of the players that were here. We had to get them thinking positive." In his efforts to build a more positive and dedicated team, Stoneman gave previously unproved players like Bengie Molina and Jared Washburn the opportunity to show themselves. In these early stages, he was patient and supportive, and that allowed these players to grow. Deciding to develop the players he already had instead of trading for more demonstrated talent may seem minor, but it communicated the implicit message to the players that the management and the coaching staff believed in them for who they were and for what they could become.

Resilience is an emotional construct, tightly tied to happiness and confidence, and Stoneman looked for ways to support his players. He took care of distractions and concerns so they could focus solely on baseball. He changed the clubhouse atmosphere, brightening up the lighting and making it a place of focus. What had once felt like a dimly lit lounge became "a place where you can prepare to do something on the field, not a place where you go to relax." Stoneman also explains that the brightly painted rocks beyond the left center field fence, part of the Disney-themed "California Spectacular" fan attraction, were toned down so that they wouldn't be disruptive to left-handed hitters. No detail was too minor when it came to changing the outlook of the Angels. Even changing their uniform had a profound impact, according to Stoneman. He goes so far as to suggest that the team's victory in the 2002 World Series was directly related to the new uniform. The old uniform had used periwinkle blue and was designed by Disney, then the team's owner. The new uniform was white with bright red details and caps, and it represented a symbolic departure from the old, mediocre Angels team.

Stoneman's support for the team, his patience with players' growth, and his focus on developing a positive environment all helped to develop the team's confidence. Studies suggest that teams with confidence put in more effort over a longer period of time than do teams that lack confidence.[8] Similarly, when you're self-confident, you're more comfortable taking the risks associated with overcoming challenges. Individuals who have reason to believe in what they're doing and in how they're doing it are more likely to take the chances needed to get to the other side of obstacles. Intuitively, the opposite is also true: if you don't believe in yourself, you're less likely to take chances.[9,10] Stoneman desperately wanted the Angels to believe in themselves because their confidence would dictate their success.

As the Angels began to grow and slowly turn around, Stoneman needed his players to band together and continue to strive for their goals. Maintaining effort is important in any endeavor, but especially in the majors. The Major League Baseball season is a long, drawn-out grind that can extend from the first week of April to the end of October, and there are many ups and downs over the course of 162 regular-season games. Resilience is about handling both the ups and the downs with

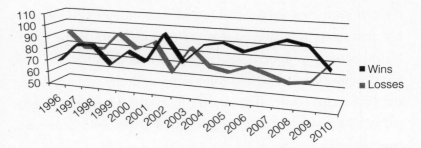

Figure 4.2. Win-Loss Records for the Los Angeles Angels, 1996–2010

grit and confidence, not allowing problems to knock you off your path. As Stoneman and the Angels progressed, they seemed to take on challenges with more and more gusto. They were becoming tough, determined, and incredibly self-assured. In short, they were becoming resilient.

As Figure 4.2 shows, Stoneman's efforts paid off. In 2002, the Angels finished the season with 99 wins and 63 losses— 4 games behind their American League (AL) West rival, the Oakland A's. They qualified for the playoffs as the league's wild card, beat the powerful New York Yankees 3 games to 1 in the American League Division Series, and then went on to beat the Minnesota Twins 4 games to 1 in the American League Championship Series.

Although they had coasted through the ALDS and the ALCS with relative ease, their World Series battle against the San Francisco Giants would prove to be an epic test of their newfound resilience. Down 3 games to 2, and in a do-or-die situation, the Angels found themselves five runs behind late in game 6. They had their backs against the wall, and yet they seemed comfortable. Rather than pack it in and go home, happy that they had overachieved during a remarkable season, they rattled off three quick runs in the bottom of the seventh inning and another three runs in the eighth, and that put them ahead for good. True to their scrappy nature, the Angels went on to win game 7 and celebrate their first World Series championship.

The 2002 season wasn't simply a one-year blip on the organization's radar. From 2003 to 2011, the Angels were one of the most successful teams in the American League, finishing first in the AL West while advancing to the playoffs five times. The Angels serve as a picture of resilience. They were a group of underrated but determined players who never backed down from a challenge, never gave in, and always believed they could achieve in spite of the obstacles.

For the Los Angeles Angels of Anaheim, the seeds of resilience may have been sown early in the turnaround process, but the Angels seemed to embrace the concept later in their development. Stoneman may have led the way with a naturally resilient disposition, but by 2002 the team had started to wholly buy in. Stoneman did not let the poor track record of the franchise deter him from taking chances on unproved but promising young guns, turning the team around, and ultimately taking the Angels to a World Series win. And the players, given the right leadership, were able to become passionate about playing baseball to the best of their ability even though they needed to overcome a decade of losses. The Angels had a sad history and a host of reasons to lose hope and back down, but ultimately they developed an unshakable belief in themselves, and that proved to be all that mattered.

THE PLAYBOOK FOR EMBRACING ADVERSITY

In spite of the pitfalls that will inevitably appear, stage IV is about seeing difficulties and drawbacks as opportunities. Challenges are moments of growth—times for you to refine yourself, make yourself better, and believe with even more confidence that you're on the right path. In the past, your team may have panicked, given up, or splintered when presented with a challenge, but by stage IV your team will unite around these tests and embrace crises as a way to strengthen and grow.

As we saw in the example of Domino's, embracing challenges as opportunities is a way to get better, learn more about yourself, and increase your focus on what is most important to you and your organization. It's a matter of perception, but team members who see hardship as a necessary means to prove themselves will inevitably move forward, whereas those who shy away from setbacks and obstacles will ultimately fall behind. In successfully working through difficulties, your team will further define itself, making itself stronger and ultimately more effective.

As your team continues to grow, an increased focus on resilience will also guide you forward, just as the Los Angeles Angels' focus on resilience made them unwilling to back down, give in, or lose. As they grew and evolved through Bill Stoneman's guidance, they found that their individual confidence, belief in each other, focus, and determination to win also grew. Taking on challenges with confidence is the mark of a resilient and successful group, and few have done it better than Stoneman and the Angels.

The resilience and the willingness to take on adversity that come with stage IV will prepare your team for the even larger challenges presented in stage V. By accepting struggle, you will push your team to get better while enhancing team members' confidence. Every fight will build team members' strength and prepare them to take on much larger obstacles.

5

Stage V:
Achieving
Success

In stage V you will finally achieve success as an organization. You and your team have overcome obstacles and achieved the goals and vision you set for yourselves and, finally, all your efforts will pay off as you become an up-and-coming industry leader, a conference or national champion, a recognized trailblazer, a great competitor. There is no denying that stage V is a stage of profound and deserved pride. You should be ecstatic, emotional, filled with the joy of success. You've reached the summit and achieved what you set out to do. This is a stage that will be remembered as one of the greatest moments of your life. The confidence you gain will stay with you forever and define how you attack challenges in the future. You've turned the organization around, and you have tangible proof that your methods and efforts have worked.

Stage V is indisputably a moment of victory, but it is also a time for much deeper contemplation—a time to embrace your newfound achievements and to consider how personal your successes have been. This is a time when you're forced to reflect on the overwhelming joy that comes with proving yourself, and on the reality of having to continue moving forward. Life doesn't stop, and success is ultimately not defined by a single achievement. Yes, you've triumphed in spite of the odds, you've worked tirelessly as a team, and you've committed to each other and the larger vision. But although these accomplishments are important and meaningful, as the celebration ends you will inevitably ask, "What's next?" When the thrill of winning subsides, you will start questioning where you are, wondering what exactly happened, and trying to find a way to continue.

Through stage V, you will adapt. As you question the direction you're moving in and work to determine where you're going to go, a new vision may ultimately emerge, along with new goals and maybe even new values. But for now, the focus is on defining who you are and adapting to where you want to go.

Both Tufts University's men's lacrosse team and iContact, an e-mail marketing software firm, have advanced through stage V in significant fashion. Guided by driven, compassionate, and contemplative leaders, Tufts lacrosse and iContact have succeeded in multiple ways, but they continue to advance by creating a distinct definition of success or adapting in an effort to be something more. Tufts lacrosse went from being one of the worst lacrosse teams in the NCAA's Division III to being an NCAA champion, and, along the way, head coach Mike Daly worked with his team to determine what success was, beyond the wins and trophies. Similarly, iContact has had tremendous success in leading a somewhat nontraditional turnaround. At one point, the corporate focus was mainly on the bottom line, but over time the company has turned its focus around, placing more attention on its environmental and social impact, and is now considered a leader among sustainable companies. The company's CEO, Ryan Allis, worked closely with his team to continually adapt to challenges, feedback, and trends. Both teams have achieved a great deal throughout their turnaround journeys, but along the way they've continually redefined success and adapted to achieve it.

DEFINE SUCCESS

The prospect of success stirs us. From Woody Allen's nonchalant perspective that "80 percent of success is showing up" to Winston Churchill's more slogging sentiment that "Success consists of going from failure to failure without loss of enthusiasm," we find inspiration in the hope that we can succeed. We read the quotes on the boardroom walls and invite the words of rallying speeches to linger long after they're said. But what is success? How do we know we've succeeded, and how do we keep success going?

The actress Carrie Fisher, of Princess Leia fame, is less quoted than Allen or Churchill but has also offered a take on success: "There is no point at which you can say, 'Well, I'm successful now. I might as well take a nap.'" For many, success is framed as a fleeting moment—the lifting of a national championship trophy, the securing of a multimillion-dollar deal, the "I do" of marriage, the final push of labor and the first cry of the baby. We think of life, our efforts, our aspirations, as something like a movie, as if we work toward the one big goal, give everything we have to a single crowning achievement, and when it's complete, the credits roll. We become so fixated on the effort to achieve that we sometimes lose sight of what we're doing and how it relates to the bigger picture. We sometimes forget that there aren't any credits, and that there's no stop to the action after we hold up the trophy. Life keeps rolling even after our big wins.

The Tufts Jumbos (as Tufts University's men's lacrosse team is called, after Jumbo the elephant, the beloved mascot of all the university's sports teams) were once a doormat in the world of lacrosse. Since the late 1990s, however, the Jumbos have undergone a breathtaking transformation that has required the team to continually redefine success in an effort to maintain its growth. Under the leadership of Mike Daly, the head coach, the Tufts men's lacrosse team has gone from being an NCAA laughingstock to being one of the most dominant teams in Division III. Along the way, Daly and his teams have established a brilliant definition of success that seems both comprehensive and profoundly transcendent of sports. Throughout their transformation, they have developed an understanding of success as something to continually strive for in all aspects of life, an ideal that they push toward every year, every practice, every day.

In the winter of 1998, when he was twenty-six years old, Daly became the unlikely head coach of the men's lacrosse team. He had never played lacrosse, and his experience as a coach was limited to a one-season stint as something of a volunteer/graduate assistant. He had played football and baseball at Tufts as an undergraduate, and upon graduation he had rolled immediately into becoming a graduate assistant in the athletic department. He pursued a master's degree in education, assisted the football team, worked in the equipment room, and made it clear that he wasn't planning on leaving the school, for which he felt a deep passion.

When he was hired as the lacrosse coach, it was as if the administration had decided to give a break to the dedicated kid who had spent many a night sleeping in the athletic department's offices. It was a kind gesture, but it couldn't objectively be argued that hiring a guy who had never played lacrosse was the best step for an ailing program. Hiring a coach with basically zero experience in the sport wasn't a recipe for epic success, and, to add to the challenge, Tufts was fielding one of the most anemic lacrosse programs in the nation, and by far the worst team in its conference. To be fair, the Jumbos were playing (and continue to play) in what is arguably the strongest Division III conference in the United States by competing in the New England Small College Athletic Conference (NESCAC), but they were seemingly incapable of winning. The year before Daly took the reins, the team had won only 2 games out of 14. The year before that, they had managed only a single win. As Daly recalls, "We hadn't had a league win in over five years, and so there were a lot of those kinds of stats that are, thankfully, a distant memory." The suffering of the Jumbos can't be overstated, and with the hiring of a dedicated guy who had no experience, it appeared that the suffering would continue.

When Daly started as lacrosse coach, he had to deal with the obvious. The players knew he lacked experience, and they questioned the hire, but Daly saw this as an opportunity. What he lacked in experience, they lacked in skill, and so the gauntlet was thrown down. Throwing and catching are fundamental skills of the game, but the players couldn't throw and catch with any consistency. They didn't practice hard, and they didn't work out with any regularity. In fact, instead of working out, players had taken to calling the desk attendant in the weight room and having him initial their sign-in sheets (a scam to get credit for lifting even when they hadn't). They put little emphasis on their lacrosse careers, preferring to focus on their studies, clubs, social life, and just about anything else. Lacrosse was an afterthought, and it showed.

To put it succinctly, the team wasn't in a position to cast stones, and so Daly bought time, using the bargaining chips the players gave him. He recalls that in those initial years there was an aura of "don't come after me until your shop is clean." He asked guys to outwork him, to get their skills to a place where they could justify criticizing him. He used his inexperience to drive them by challenging them to work as hard as he did and improve at his rate. Daly pushed the players to take responsibility for themselves while he gobbled up everything he could about lacrosse by meeting with Division I coaches, attending camps, breaking down historic games, and hitting conferences and professional lectures.

Aside from their lack of effort and work ethic, Daly was most surprised by the players' lack of passion for the game they devoted so much of their time to. As someone who had had an amazing experience playing sports, Daly remembers this absence of passion as the thing that pained him most. "There just wasn't a lot of love of lacrosse," he says. "There weren't guys who were lacrosse junkies. Some played for a lot of reasons, but none of them really included that true love of the game. It wasn't the best two hours of their day. In most cases, it was some of the worst two hours of their day." And so, in addition to pushing the players to work hard, develop their skills, and learn more about the game, Daly also tried to instill the love and passion that would drive guys to go out and be their best.

He stacked copies of *Inside Lacrosse* in his office, encouraged guys to come by and watch game film, kept his door open, ordered extra gear like gloves and bags and shirts and shorts, and started giving the players reasons to fall in love with what they were doing. It didn't take long before the fire was burning. In his first year, the team went out and nabbed its first league win in years by beating Trinity College. It was as if they had done the impossible. Little ol' Tufts, coached by a guy who barely knew the sport, went out and won a game in the toughest conference in the nation. By every measure, the players had succeeded. They had made massive strides in an incredibly short amount of time, and they had every reason to be ecstatic about their progress. They threw their equipment and cheered, and they ran onto the field as the game clock ran down. They celebrated as if they had won a championship. They had made a monumental stride forward, and by all accounts they had succeeded wildly, but they wouldn't stop there.

A single league win, even the first in years, is far from a league championship or even a winning record, but it was a start. More important, the win was the result of the many small seeds that Daly was constantly sowing—the hard work, the passion, the magazines, and the gear. Now that the seeds were taking root, Daly and his team were eager to see them grow. As you can imagine, Daly and the Tufts Jumbos didn't pack up after beating Trinity in 1999. They didn't capture the moment with a marble statue or even commission a sketch of the fateful win. Instead, they built on it. They celebrated the hard-fought victory but then went back to work with a renewed focus and new understanding of what they could accomplish.

Success is oftentimes wrongly associated with external gains, such as social standing, a high profile, an influential job title, a trophy that proves one team is better than its opponent, or a car that symbolizes wealth. But success is actually something much more personal, reflecting an internal commitment to specific values, characteristics, and beliefs.[1] Success comes from helping others, from being the best you can be through fair and considerate participation, from a commitment to honesty and integrity, and from giving everything you have to achieving a specific goal. In this sense, success varies from person to person, and although more external measures of success do exist, they become much less important to the individual striving to attain a personal ideal.

As the Tufts Jumbos continued to move forward, they began to think further about what success meant to them. They talked about it as a team and began believing that success really wasn't about single wins and might not even be about trophies and individual honors. "We talked about the mundanity of excellence," Daly explains. "We always think of Olympic gold medal winners as these Greek gods, when in fact they're just normal ugly people, just like us, who work really, really hard and, more importantly, work really, really hard on the really, really little things." And so the Jumbos set out to be just that—a team of normal ugly people who work really, really hard on the little things. In time, the members of the lacrosse team began to view success as the pride that comes with working obsessively on the details, with being the best they could be in every way possible.

They placed a unique focus on preparation and became the fittest team at the school. They pushed each other to get better and slowly improved their skills. Promising players became attracted to the new ethic. New recruits meant more talent, more competition, and more intense workouts. The team was growing, improving, and advancing, and Daly was pushing along the way. There were new helmets, team-issued workout shirts, and top-of-the-line equipment—the small rewards for the price of commitment. As the minutes and hours, days and years of effort ticked by, the Tufts Jumbos grew into a top-flight program, but there was more to it. Sure, they started to win, but that wasn't their only measure of triumph. It wasn't just the on-field wins that were defining their success.

They took pride in being students at one of the premier academic institutions in the world. They challenged each other to get good grades, in addition to goals and assists. They set their sights on careers that demanded a distinct blend of excellence, careers that honored the values they associated with Tufts lacrosse, values such as effort, sacrifice, and commitment. Some went into the military, pursuing Officer Candidate School. Some volunteered with service programs. Others dove into teaching and coaching. More and more people started to linger around the program. From administrators to parents and alumni, Daly was welcoming new faces to practice and games, shaking hands at national events, and encouraging the involvement of anyone willing to commit to the team.

Success became more and more personal and increasingly specific. Beyond successes that were occurring on the field, in the classroom, and in careers, Daly and the players included relationships in their equation of what it meant to be a success. They began to identify with certain types of people, highlighting specific traits in the friends that surrounded them as ideals worth striving for. Of the many who deserve highlighting, Daly points to Mark Doughtie and Julio Quintanilla as two people who embody such ideals. Doughtie, the lacrosse team's athletic trainer, was awarded the Bronze Star during his service in Vietnam. Quite possibly more bear than man, Doughtie is the type of guy who hurts your back when he slaps it and cracks your hand when he shakes it. He's strong and intimidating but oozes an approachable toughness. He is emotional in a way that is wholly unpredictable from his appearance, and his loyalty seems to set a bar for what the word means. Similarly, Daly points to Quintanilla, a custodian for the university and one of the most significant supporters of the program. Daly explains, "He's here at seven o'clock every morning, works until three o'clock, comes out to our practice, leaves our practice for his six-to-midnight shift, and just does it every single day, and does it for whatever his wages are, and is just happy to have the opportunity." In contrast to Doughtie, Quintanilla is a wisp of a figure but recognizably proud. His dark black hair is well gelled, his smile beams, and his shoulders are indefatigably sturdy.

Quintanilla and Doughtie inspire the Tufts team. They represent a level of success that Daly not only respects but also hopes that every athlete he coaches is willing to aim for. Quintanilla and Doughtie are hardworking, tough, compassionate, loyal—good people. Daly says of Quintanilla, "We always reflect on and point to Julio's work ethic, to Julio's dedication to his family back in El Salvador." You won't find Julio Quintanilla's name on the Tufts website, but he works as hard as any professor, coach, or administrator to make Tufts one of the best universities in the nation. Doughtie is also unheralded but equally dedicated to doing his part. By focusing on the traits of these two men and others, Daly and his team have set an additional bar for what it means to be successful, once again suggesting that the success of the Tufts lacrosse team is measured by factors that are far more significant than any single win or on-field triumph. Success is about family, loyalty, effort, and much, much more.

In addition to focusing on relationships, schoolwork, hard work, and personal development, Daly and his team also developed a unique understanding of the skills and strategy that would lead to on-field success. They challenged conventional thinking in lacrosse and continue to tweak a quirky style of play that demands impeccably conditioned athletes playing at a breakneck pace. They adjusted their practices to emphasize specific skills (shooting, conditioning, fast breaks, and so on) needed for their style. Daly began reading books about strategy and coaching while also drawing on his degree in education and his interest in human development. Daly and his players asked each other what needed to get better and how improvement could happen, and they even began to experiment with emphasizing the off-field intangibles that everyone talks about but few people practice. "The leadership changes every year," Daly says, "and what do we do to truly educate our guys on leadership?" The answer was "nothing," and Daly questioned that logic. Coaches spoke at national conventions, arguing that bad seasons were often due to a dearth of leadership, whereas a season's success was contingent on the leadership of upperclassmen. Knowing a good coach wouldn't take the field without practicing offensive plays that would be critical to the success of his team, Daly resolved to set aside time to practice leadership. Friday afternoons are now a designated training time, when groups of teammates gather for lunch to discuss assigned chapters from books that Daly considers critical.

The Tufts Jumbos' transformation took around ten years to complete, and throughout that period Daly unquestionably embraced a profound and evolving sense of success. For Daly, his staff, and his players, the progression was slow but peppered with memorable moments and scintillating achievements. "It's such a blessing and a curse," he admits. "We lament so much harder on the losses than we even remotely think about enjoying any of the successes." But he stays committed to the climb, to the process of advancement, and continues plodding forward, redefining what success is along the way.

The growth of his team has been physically captured in his office, adorned with posters, signed pictures, letters from politicians and NFL owners, All-American plaques, and program awards. The small space is a virtual museum, dedicated to one program's growth from afterthought to contender. Outside his office are bulletin boards crowded with newspaper and magazine articles, stories about the young men who have played lacrosse at Tufts and about their on-field achievements, the distinctions they've earned in the military, the community service projects they've led, and the time they've spent helping others while learning more about themselves.

In 2010, Daly and his team won the Division III national championship. They achieved the ultimate measure of success a collegiate team can achieve. With a record of 20 and 1, they became the only Tufts University athletic team ever to win an NCAA championship. They had come out of nowhere. As Figure 5.1 shows, they rose up from nothing and became

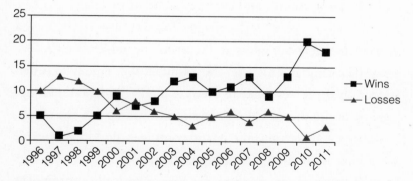

Figure 5.1. Wins, Losses, and Postseason Achievement for Tufts University Lacrosse Team, 1996–2011

Table 5.1. Details of Tufts University Lacrosse Team's Performance, 1999–2011

Year	Wins	Losses	Comments
1999	5	10	Mike Daly's first year
2000	9	6	
2001	7	8	
2002	8	6	NESCAC, first round
2003	12	5	NESCAC, championship game, runner-up
2004	13	3	NESCAC, semifinal
2005	10	5	NESCAC, first round
2006	11	6	NESCAC, first round
2007	13	4	NCAA tournament, second round
2008	9	6	NESCAC, first round
2009	13	5	NCAA, first round
2010	20	1	NCAA, champion
2011	18	3	NCAA championship game, runner-up

the most successful lacrosse team in the nation, and they followed up in 2011 with a remarkable trip back to the NCAA championship game, where they suffered a disappointing loss (see Table 5.1 for additional details about the team's record from 1999 to 2011). In a photo taken after the 2011 setback, Daly, holding the runner-up trophy, looks like he's battling an aggressive parasite. He's disappointed, hurt, pissed. And so it goes—the Jumbos are one of the top teams in the nation, but there's more to achieve, more success to define and pursue.

For Daly and his team, as you might guess, the drive hasn't waned. And so what do we make of success? What do we do with the reality that life doesn't stop in light of our achievements? At this stage of an organization's turnaround, success is a standard to continually live up to. For Daly and the Jumbos, you keep slugging, keep striving, keep working to get better, and never stop thinking about what success genuinely means. The achievement of winning an NCAA championship was certainly celebrated as an incredible accomplishment, but it now serves as a foundation on which to build more success, proof that the simple formula of working hard toward specific goals can have its rewards. External success is fleeting and fickle, and at this stage that's obvious. Achievement came to Daly and the Tufts lacrosse team, but it didn't slow them down. If anything, it's refocused them, reminding them that dreams are not only worth working for, they can also come true.

ADAPT

The story of the Tufts University men's lacrosse team shows us that we never stop working, even after we've accomplished our goals. We continually redefine success, making it a personal set of ideals to constantly strive toward. Whereas Tufts has shown us that success is ever-changing, iContact teaches us the value of adapting to renewed standards and expectations. As a small start-up that was succeeding in growth and profits, iContact could have continued on a prosperous path, but the company redefined what success should be and then adapted to the challenge. It changed itself and became a leader in sustainable business practices.

As you succeed and refine your understanding of what success means, you must also adapt. The game keeps changing, and your ability to adjust to new rules and goals will define your capacity to achieve, moving forward. Change is essential, and if you don't push yourself to adapt, you're likely to stop achieving. As Batman once told Robin in a moment of invaluable insight, "An investigative mind and physical skills are just tools. The most important weapon in your arsenal will be your ability to adapt."[2] Adapting to the situation, changing in an effort to stay on top, may in fact be one of the most important tools in your arsenal, and few stories are as intriguing as the story of iContact.

In July of 2003, iContact began as an e-mail marketing software company, committed to the long-term vision of building "a great global company based here in North Carolina for our customers, employees, and community." In the early going, a core group focused on slow growth. iContact then ballooned from a small company to a moderate-size organization in only a couple of years. iContact was advancing according to plan, growing in revenue and adding employees, but the plan didn't seem to capture where the company should go. To the iContact founders, measuring growth solely through financial numbers and employee count was what other organizations had always done, and it seemed specious.

The world was changing. Thomas Friedman, in a December 2006 op-ed piece for the *New York Times,* echoed the sentiments and observations of many when he wrote, "We reached a tipping point this year—where living, acting, designing, investing and manufacturing green came to be understood by a critical mass of citizens, entrepreneurs and officials as the most patriotic, capitalistic, geopolitical, healthy and competitive thing they could do. Hence my own motto: 'Green is the new red, white, and blue.'"[3] A year later, one of the most disastrous recessions in history struck, and midsize companies like iContact began pondering their fate, wondering how they'd stay relevant and alive.

Around 2007, in an effort to keep his organization alive and growing in a shifting landscape, iContact CEO Ryan Allis was crafting a broader plan for the burgeoning tech firm. Allis saw a play, one that was not only sensible and reflective of the changing times but also something he was truly passionate about. Allis's business partner, the cofounder of iContact, had been fighting cancer during this period. Ultimately he survived, but he and Allis had been spending time discussing the importance of making an impact, staying true to yourself, and making the most of life. And so, in an effort to adapt to what businesses could and perhaps should be, Allis dedicated iContact to a more sustainable path. Allis began to consider the organization as a vehicle for positive impact, as a means of doing good for the community and the environment while also making money.

In spite of his hopes, Allis found himself struggling to find a way for iContact to serve others in a more beneficent manner. E-mail marketing is a lauded and necessary service, but it's not digging wells for African villages or providing food for the Appalachian needy. Allis explains, "We were just a normal company. We very much cared about customers, employees, community, but we didn't have an integrated philanthropic program." In spite of this obvious obstacle, Allis was undaunted, believing that iContact could be transformed into a more philanthropic and environmentally conscious organization.

Allis has always found ways to get things done, and he fully expected to do the same with this particular project. When he was eighteen years old, he wrote the book *Zero to One Million: How to Build a Company to $1 Million in Sales,* which, as the title suggests, chronicles his entrepreneurial efforts to grow a $1 million company from nothing in fourteen months. He also started iContact in 2003, when he was about nineteen, and knew nothing but success with the firm, growing it to a multimillion-dollar enterprise, with hundreds of employees and thousands of clients, in only a few years. Allis made things happen. But this wasn't about starting up. This was about change.

Allis started with a simple challenge to himself and his organization: to do more. And, as with most of what he has set his mind to, his goals were quickly achieved. He had already been involved in service-oriented nonprofits and had been acting as an angel investor for socially responsible organizations. Now he had to filter his enthusiasm and passion for such causes through iContact. Slowly advancements were made. In 2010, Matt Kopac, a recent graduate of the Yale School of Management, was brought in to assume the title of corporate responsibility manager. The now midsize tech company was committed not only to offering top-notch e-mail marketing services globally but also to being an industry leader in social and environmental sustainability. iContact was adapting—adjusting to a shifting global trend, a changing environment.

One concept that has emerged in an effort to offer structure to companies like iContact, companies that are working to have a broader positive impact through business, is the Benefit Corporation, or B Corporation. B Corporations represent a new era of business maintenance and progress, "a new type of corporation which uses the power of business to solve social and environmental problems."[4] These organizations are more tightly monitored than most other corporations, welcoming stricter standards and guidelines in an effort to more proactively contribute to sustainable business practices. In many ways, these organizations are leading a dramatic shift in corporate philosophy and practice, and iContact wanted to join the party. Kopac, iContact's new corporate responsibility manager, assumed early responsibility for making iContact a certified B Corporation. The process was rigorous, calling for increased accountability when it came to measuring social and environmental practices. Nevertheless, Kopac says, "having the framework of the B Corp certification was really helpful for our team members to understand what it meant to be a triple-bottom-line company, and it also helped us to be able to measure our success at achieving that goal." With the full support of Allis, Kopac set out to push iContact to adapt further and become B Corporation–certified, a recognized triple-bottom-line company.

The term *triple bottom line* has come to capture the intersection of corporate practice with social and ecological impact, and this concept has become increasingly influential in recent years. A triple bottom line essentially offers an accountability strategy whereby organizations can quantify not only their profits but also their social and environmental impacts. Specifically, the three distinct areas of organizational impact measured with the triple-bottom-line approach are the three P's: profits, people (society), and planet (environment).[5] Any company looking to be more sustainable needs to pay attention to the triple bottom line, and this is especially true for a company looking to attain certification as a B Corporation.

In early 2010, the first time iContact applied for the certification, the company didn't hit the mark. Organizations are assessed by an independent third-party rater on such variables as accountability and transparency, commitment to the community, and environmental impact. (For those interested, www.bcorporation.net offers information about third-party raters and the overall process.) For an organization to be certified as a B Corporation, it needs to score 80 points or more out of a possible 200. After iContact's first failure, Kopac and the company pored over the feedback and critically assessed where iContact's efforts could be made better for the next try.

In June of 2010, only three months after that initial failure, iContact was awarded certification as a B Corporation. iContact was now one of a small number of North Carolina businesses to have attained such certification, and it was the only such company in the e-mail marketing industry. Furthermore, by working together through the certification process, the members of the iContact team had not only adapted to the new requirements for a B Corporation but also increased their awareness of the positive social and environmental impacts that iContact could have. As Allis explains, "There was that sense that we really were taking significant, real actions on social and environmental responsibility. I think that people got a sense that our company's mission was more than just about making money, but it was rather about making money while doing good." iContact had adapted by leading a dramatic turnaround focused on sustainability and was using the organization to leave a positive and powerful legacy.

According to Martin Reeves and Mike Deimler, senior partners and managing directors at the Boston Consulting Group, "Globalization, new technologies and greater transparency have combined to upend the business environment and give many CEOs a deep sense of unease."[6] They go on to outline four "abilities" considered necessary to adapt to a new or changing environment:

1. Identifying and reacting to pertinent information
2. Experimenting
3. Managing complex systems
4. Thinking adaptively across organizational levels

Companies and teams focused on forward movement think and act in these terms. They are constantly filtering information to identify strategic advantages, are willing to experiment with adaptive concepts and ideas, and are capable of managing a variety of systems while pushing decisions and actions throughout the organization. An adaptive culture facilitates quick movement, creativity, and fluid decision making that will likely support larger trends while benefiting the advancement and progress of the organization.

Interestingly, iContact seems to have embodied much of what Reeves and Deimler outline. First, Allis absorbed the many cues that corporate sustainability was more than a passing fad. He embraced the concept as a means to strategically position iContact in a space of its own while also defining iContact as a conscientious organization focused on doing the right thing. Then Allis began experimenting, first by creating a new position to oversee the organization's sustainability efforts and then by giving Kopac free rein to carve a new and unique path. As iContact's sustainability efforts continue to advance, Allis and Kopac are regularly working with a variety of interconnected systems and are encouraging others to think adaptively and creatively. For example, employee action teams have been developed, and they meet monthly to brainstorm and discuss potential sustainability efforts. These teams are composed of employees across departments, are led by conscientious volunteers, and have brought about an increase in employee engagement and empowerment. Although iContact set out to achieve certification as a B Corporation, the company has actually launched an internal initiative that is defining both what the organization has become and where it is going.

The goal of B Corporation certification was once seen as an end in itself but is now considered to have been a definitive beginning. iContact is just starting its journey as a sustainable organization with a commitment to a triple bottom line. In the year following its receipt of B Corporation status, the employee action teams offered quarterly training programs for nonprofit organizations interested in advancing sustainability efforts. In addition, Kopac explains, as "an example on the environmental side, we realized we weren't doing that well in terms of sorting waste, recycling from landfill waste. So we had an idea from the group to centralize our recycling, and so we revamped our recycling process internally." From creating in-house action teams that have addressed the needs of regional nonprofit organizations to revamping the company's internal recycling program, iContact is making strides but is also very much beginning its adaptive journey as a more sustainable and conscientious enterprise.

Kopac is clear that iContact's efforts to advance and adapt are far from over. He says, "To manage a triple bottom line, you can't just have some good initiatives going. I think you not only have to have goals relating to sustainability, you have to act on those goals, you have to evaluate yourself on those goals. We put out a corporate responsibility report a couple months ago," he adds, describing the types of goals that iContact is now considering, "where we laid out goals for ourselves on a variety of social and environmental metrics, where we're evaluating ourselves." He notes that this "is something that didn't even exist a year and half ago." For Kopac, Allis, and the larger iContact team, efforts to monitor the company's triple bottom line are just beginning, and their willingness to adapt will continue to move them forward. As the team stays focused on establishing goals, monitoring progress, and adjusting for continued success, iContact's sustainability efforts will continue to flourish.

iContact continues to grow in profits and outreach. This growth is certainly a function of hard work, but the company's success in turning its sustainability efforts around was largely determined by a willingness to adapt. iContact adapted to a larger, changing world, and the organization is changing itself as it strives to be the best it can be. iContact was already a company on the rise, a genuine success story, but the company knew it could do better. By adapting its focus and dedicating itself to a more sustainable path, iContact continues to evolve as it reaches for unimagined heights.

THE PLAYBOOK FOR
ACHIEVING SUCCESS

In stage V you will win, achieve, and accomplish exactly what you and your team set out to do. Yet, as you slowly check off the goals you once conscientiously and determinedly set, you will begin to establish new expectations for what is possible. The race isn't over, even after you cross the finish line. Evolution is necessary for continued growth, and so you must continually redefine what success means for you and your team. Success will become a compilation of ideals to strive for, as opposed to the achievement of any one goal or victory.

You and your team will also need to adapt. Adaptation is an essential part of your growth and long-term success. Keep an eye on the horizon, notice trends in your industry and the larger environment, work to stay fresh and ahead of the curve, and challenge yourself, but also invite the ideas of others. In order to continually guide your team forward, you will need to create an environment that promotes and encourages functional and healthy change.

As you work through stage V, don't take your victories lightly. Celebrate, be proud, and recognize your triumphs for what they are, but don't lose sight of tomorrow. Even the biggest win today can become obsolete if you do not continue to push your team forward. Just as with the Tufts Jumbos and iContact, sustained success is contingent on reevaluating what success means and adapting along the way. Achievements are important and vital to the momentum and growth of your team, but keep pushing forward, raising the bar, and making the necessary changes to continually meet those new expectations.

6

Stage VI: Nurturing a Culture of Excellence

Once you've reached stage VI, you're an indisputable winner. The turnaround is complete. It's not to say that you won't go through some hard times. No matter how good you become, you and your team will occasionally face setbacks. But stage VI is about bracing for those times by developing a winning culture that is both lasting and enduring. Everyone dips. You'll have a losing season or a bad year, but winning organizations find ways to carry on and triumph in spite of the inevitable pitfalls. Organizations that reach stage VI have done so because they maintain a level of long-standing excellence that comes to define them. Over time, they succeed, and even when they fail, they recover quickly, turning back to their winning ways before losing takes hold.

Along with focusing on developing a culture that can withstand performance dips, an organization at stage VI needs to concentrate on continual learning and innovation. Culture, continual learning, and innovation are ever present throughout the Team Turnaround Process but are often over-shadowed by more prominent themes during the first five stages. Think back to stage I, when Jeffrey Lurie, Frank Esposito, and David Helfer worked to learn about the faults of their respective organizations; stage II, when Jim Grundberg defined the guiding values for SeeMore Putters; stage III, when Marilyn Masaitis visited her customer at home to learn why he had stopped patronizing her restaurant; stage IV, when Domino's Pizza creatively utilized social media; and stage V, when coach Mike Daly implemented formal leadership educa-tion for his Tufts University lacrosse players. Each of these actions not only helped to develop a winning culture but also represented a leader's effort to learn and innovate. And so we come to stage VI, where culture, continual learning, and innovation must move from the background and take center stage.

Teams that reach stage VI are few and far between because it takes enormous amounts of discipline to maintain the high standards necessary for constant growth. As you enter stage VI, you must push yourself to continue to grow and evolve while you also nurture the culture that has been built. Stage VI organizations are the dynasties, the pacesetters, the standard makers. Two examples of organizations that have reached this stage are the Montgomery County (Maryland) Public School system and the Pittsburgh Steelers.

Not only did Jerry Weast guide Montgomery County Public Schools (MCPS) through a breathtaking turnaround with a compulsive focus on continual learning and innovation, his constant attention to these variables also positioned the district for sustained improvement. Weast took charge of an organization that, on the surface, appeared successful. By most measures, the district was a solid performer, achieving well on standardized tests and sending a considerable number of graduates to fine colleges and universities. But Weast looked past the façade of feel-good success stories and discovered a district poised for a precipitous decline. He studied, he learned, and, through a brilliant and innovative effort, he rebuilt the foundation of his organization, made it stronger, and implemented systems and processes that would allow the district to continue to learn and grow long after he was gone. Now MCPS serves as an example—a standard for how public schools can be run and for what they are capable of achieving.

In similar fashion, Dan Rooney, once president and chairman of the Pittsburgh Steelers, positioned his organization for continued success. Under the long-standing leadership of Rooney, the Steelers have become one of the most successful franchises in all of sports, and the organization's culture is something to marvel at. Rooney never set out to have just a single winning season. Instead, he set his sights on winning continuously, on regularly competing for championships, year after year. You may see this as a seemingly minor distinction, but for the Steelers it has made all the difference. The culture of the Steelers has been established with the long term in mind. The franchise is a future-oriented organization, one that is focused as much on winning tomorrow as on winning today. The culture has evolved and strengthened with time and is now as strong as the name it bears, taking on challenge after challenge with the full expectation of coming out on top, enduring, and further emboldening itself.

The Montgomery County Public School system and the Pittsburgh Steelers have both proved themselves winners, but it's their long-standing commitment to success that's of note. As you lead your organization through this final stage, pay close attention to the details—those little efforts that make up the big picture. Focus on continual learning and innovation, and work to develop a strong and lasting culture of success.

CONTINUE LEARNING AND INNOVATING

Those who achieve over and over, the genuine winners, never stop learning and never stop innovating. Organizations that stay at the top are always growing, always pushing, always striving to be just a little better, just a little more accomplished or proficient. Thanks to Jerry Weast, this is very much true of the Montgomery County Public School System.

Jerry Weast is a decorated and revered superintendent who has garnered the attention of business and academic leaders alike. He served as MCPS superintendent for twelve years and retired from his post in June 2011. He ran his organization with finesse and grit, constantly demanding growth by instilling an insatiable hunger for learning and innovation. Weast's value to education is unmatched. He's the Michael Jordan, Johnny Unitas, and Wayne Gretzky of superintendents. He began as a superintendent when he was only twenty-eight years old, worked in five different states, and oversaw eight different school districts, but it was his work with Montgomery County, Maryland, that sealed his legacy.

MCPS is one of the twenty largest school districts in the United States, serving more than 144,000 students, employing more than 22,000 professionals, and, as of 2011, managing a $2.1 billion operating budget. In addition to being the largest school system in Maryland, the Montgomery County school system is also the state's most diverse. A suburb of Washington, D.C., Montgomery County is home to a broad swath of cultural and socioeconomic types. The student population speaks nearly two hundred languages, and 13 percent receive English for Speakers of Other Languages (ESOL) services. In addition, students in the county come from more than 160 countries, and more than 30 percent of the students receive subsidized meals.

When Weast first took over as superintendent in 1999, by all public accounts MCPS was successful. According to standardized tests, grades, college admissions, and other metrics, the students of Montgomery County were statistically succeeding. MCPS was meeting state standards, and students were graduating, but Weast needed to learn more. In his efforts to better understand the statistics, he uncovered a reality that gave him reason for concern. As Weast explains, "We [essentially] had two districts, both of them large districts, both of them around 70,000 in size. One of them held almost 80 percent African American and Latino [students]. And the other one had 80 percent white and Asian [students]." The African American and Latino region was more of a transient/rental community, smaller in geographical scope, blighted with poverty, and generally underperforming academically. In contrast, the largely white and Asian region was more affluent, had deeper community roots, and statistically inflated the entire school district in terms of academic achievement. Nevertheless, although the district was relying on around 20 percent of its students' achievements to satisfy state and national expectations and mandates, the high-performing Asian and white population was diminishing in size, yielding to the ballooning populations of African American and Latino families. Something had to be done to instill equity in the community, not just to ensure that the county could continue to report positive academic statistics but also to properly serve the growing population of underserved children who deserved a strong preparatory education.

Weast was right to be concerned by what he had uncovered, and he knew that MCPS's outward appearances of success presented a significant obstacle. Success, even the perception of success, can be a dangerous thing. When teams win, they can become complacent. Success feels good and builds confidence, but it can also breed sloppy habits, overconfidence, and eventual performance decline. By contrast, failure can be easy to learn from. If you lose, your mistakes are apparent, and you're forced to learn from them if you ever want to get better. For organizations that sustain success over the long haul, learning must come in times of success as well as in times of failure.[1] In fact, there's evidence that exploring successes along with failures leads to sustained and continual achievement. Weast understood this. It was the principle that had guided his discovery that the district was actually in decline, and it would be the principle that would now guide the district through remarkable growth.

Given the reality that Weast had unearthed, he was committed to change. The underserved African American and Latino communities needed more assistance and attention. Their populations were beginning to swell throughout the county, and if the academic focus didn't shift to a more comprehensive model that targeted their development and achievement, the district would inevitably suffer. He was sold on the need to reduce the achievement gap, but he would have to sell the larger team on it as well, and that included scads of teachers and administrators as well as students and parents. Weast was cognizant that the high-performing teachers and administrators could easily point the finger at their low-performing counterparts, and he needed to create a compelling argument that would spur both groups to action. He set out to frame his argument in a way that would resonate with the low- as well as the high-performing elements of his district, and he hoped the larger team would buy in.

As Weast developed his pitch, he knew that the moral play was to offer equal academic opportunities to all students. He also knew that the moral play wouldn't pack the needed punch. Rather than focus on what was right, he put his energy into the less obvious but arguably more effective case, centering his argument on convincing stakeholders (teachers, principals, parents, and the business community) that change was an economic necessity. Weast suggested that the school district was a single brand that attracted new families, businesses, and opportunities to the community, and he made it clear that the brand was in serious jeopardy. "We studied other organizations that turned around," Weast explains. "They had to have a common element. They had to have a brand. 'The Montgomery County Public Schools Way,' if you will." The brand needed protection. Property values, business interests, and general quality of life were likely to decline if the low-performing student population continued to envelop the high-performing student group.

He framed the problem as a countywide crisis that couldn't be denied by any single racial or socioeconomic group. Weast argued that everyone shared the issue because if the school system didn't improve, the county would be seen as less attractive for businesses and homebuyers, and the existing value of property owned by current residents would degrade. It was a clear financial issue that relied on the "we're only as strong as our weakest link" argument. In essence, Weast was suggesting that if the performance of low academic achievers was not raised, the county population would change, the attractiveness of the county would decline, and residents would ultimately lose money. It was hard not to buy in. Administrators, teachers, parents, and students came on board in a short amount of time and committed to the vision of overcoming the existing challenge. Weast says, "I wanted 80 percent of kids college-ready by 2014." The county committed to improving the performance of underachieving students and to universally raising the bar for every student in the district.

Once the mandate was identified, Weast and the district focused on their new vision. In working to achieve it, Weast stuck with his commitment to continual education. Just as he himself had originally spent time poring over statistics and identifying the district's unsustainable achievement gap—the issue that now seemed so significant—he now asked administrators, teachers, parents, and students to adopt a similar lust for learning. He asked them to give their opinions, to hear out other stakeholders, and to challenge him and each other as necessary. If the district was going to advance, everyone would have to be responsible for pushing it forward, but for that to happen, everyone would have to learn more about teaching, education, and one another.

Weast and the county set out to learn more about what they needed to do in order to better serve the underserved students and narrow the existing achievement gap. He says, "With the students, we listened and surveyed. With the parents, we listened and surveyed. With the teachers, we listened and surveyed." He asked people to describe what they were experiencing in the trenches. He asked where things were going well, and where improvements could be made. "When we make mistakes," he told them, "we're going to tell it first, tell it loud, and tell it often, and we're going to learn from them." Mistakes and failures became tools of learning. Weast put his focus on the potential of errors to teach people a better and more effective manner of doing things, and more and more teachers and administrators began talking and learning from each other.

Beyond the surveys and conversations, which were primarily serving teachers and administrators, Weast also developed learning opportunities for families and parents. He was concerned with the lack of awareness and the passivity of some of the parents in the lower socioeconomic groups, and he responded by reaching out to them. Weast explains, "We created study circles. We created academic academies to train parents how to work the system." Weast went into the areas of the county that needed help the most, and he opened the communication channels between parents and school personnel. Through the study circles and academies, the administration asked for critical feedback while also educating parents about the differences between strong and ineffective teachers. Weast and MCPS used this feedback, and they partnered with the teachers' and principals' unions to devise a way to eliminate poorly performing teachers and administrators. According to Weast, more than five hundred employees have been eliminated for performance-related reasons. Through this process, the school system began to become a cohesive community, working toward the goal of making 80 percent of its students college-ready by 2014.

As if engaging administrators, teachers, and families in the learning process wasn't enough, Weast looked even further. He stretched beyond the world of education, eager to learn from other fields. Weast figured that a number of industries might have insights into best practices and general management philosophy that could be helpful to Montgomery County. He acted on the hunch and invited thirty-seven businesses active in Montgomery County to develop a nonprofit entity that would work alongside the school system to advance professional development and other causes. He recalls, "We organized the business community, not to give us money but actually to give us brand power." Businesses such as United HealthCare, PricewaterhouseCoopers, Lockheed Martin, and NASDAQ signed on to offer insight into management, systems, and organizational success. "I [worked] with them personally," Weast says, "and then I [had] my top team work with them, and we put their team and our team together." For example, United HealthCare had significant experience in implementing

Six Sigma, a theoretical and practical approach to improving business processes, and the company helped train MCPS on how to do the same. Essentially, Weast looked to members of the local business community to help his leadership team become more familiar with accepted management practices and leadership development strategies, leaning on them as consultants as he and his team made and implemented critical decisions. The effort proved brilliant, original, and innovative.

Guided by what they had learned, the team members in the district kept moving forward. Along the way, they developed an insatiable hunger to discover more about each other, about what needed to be done, and about the general process of education. As they increased their awareness, not only were individual students assisted, key innovations also began to evolve. Among the many innovative efforts that were made, Weast's reorganization of the central office and his reconsideration of traditional measures of student achievement proved a symbolic and strategic shift of considerable note. He explains, "We had to become more of a support network to the field and change the unit of change from a bunch of test scores to each individual classroom." No longer would averaged scores on standardized tests serve as an adequate measure of the progress of individual students. Instead, Weast and other administrators encouraged teachers to look past scores on standardized tests and focus on the learning experiences in individual classrooms. This was a colossal change in mind-set, a move away from spotlighting collective statistics and toward placing more emphasis on individual classroom experience.

By reorienting the school system's focus on each student's developmental experience, the team members freed themselves up to make even more innovative and critical changes. They established a new standard for success, developing metrics that were far more comprehensive and demanding than those imposed by the State of Maryland or by the nation. Maryland's state-level educational guidelines ultimately measured success on the basis of whether a student graduated from high school, but Weast and his colleagues wanted MCPS students to succeed in college. Therefore, through research, they learned about key indicators throughout a student's career that predicted success in college. From these, they established their seven keys to college readiness, clear guidelines that constitute a standard unequivocally higher than the State of Maryland's. These keys include specific achievements in the primary grades, ranging from reading at an advanced level in kindergarten and grade 2 to student participation in advanced mathematics in grade 5.[2] They started looking at more refined areas of learning, and they placed considerable emphasis on the early grades, knowing that, for most students, long-term achievement is rooted in the early years.

With the help of administrators and teachers throughout the county, Weast boldly slashed $60 to $80 million in ineffective programs. The move was somewhat counterintuitive. Would slashing established programs truly help the students? Weast explains that these programs "sounded good and looked good on a brochure but had low volume, marginal quality, and actually didn't do anything except make the person delivering them feel good." By getting rid of them, he freed the budget up, and that money could now be used to support a smaller student-to-teacher ratio throughout the district. Weast and his team worked to keep classroom sizes in effective schools the same, and they used the newfound money to reduce classroom sizes in less effective schools. In addition, the real-located funds allowed them to place greater emphasis on early childhood education, "especially for the kids in poverty," Weast explains. The expectation was that long-term outcomes would depend on putting critical resources into the early years of education. The foundation for continued excellence was being built, and students would grow through a system that caught them early and developed them from the early grades through graduation from high school. Figure 6.1 shows the narrowing achievement gap among African American,

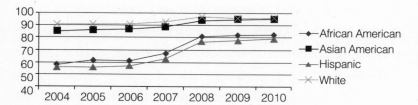

Figure 6.1. Percentage of Montgomery County (Maryland) Seventh-Grade Students, by Ethnicity, Scoring "Proficient" or "Advanced" in Reading, 2004–2010
Source: www.mdreportcard.org

Asian American, Hispanic, and white students during Jerry Weast's tenure.

The most innovative executives are tireless in their questioning of the status quo, and Weast's efforts, from creating parent academies to building relationships with local businesses, were well outside the accepted norm. Leaders who drive innovation observe customers and other stakeholders to better understand their behaviors and needs, and they experiment with new ideas.[3] By doing just that, Weast ushered in systemic changes that would provide the larger organization with valuable feedback for years to come.

Weast drove change where the school system was weakest. He looked to the underserved, and the result of his attempt to innovatively improve education for the county's at-need populations was widespread, sustained success. The outcomes have been stunning. There has been a wide array of academic achievements in the Montgomery County Public School system; here are just a few:

- In 2010, MCPS won the prestigious Malcolm Baldridge National Quality Award, the highest presidential honor given to American organizations for performance excellence in the business, health care, education, and nonprofit sectors.
- MCPS achieved the highest graduation rate of the nation's fifty largest school systems for three years in a row (2009–2011).

- MCPS had the most high schools in the nation's top 100 high schools, as ranked by *Newsweek* in June 2010.
- Each of MCPS's 25 high schools made *Newsweek*'s list of America's Best High Schools in 2010, representing the nation's top 1,622 high schools (the top 6 percent).
- In 2010, 50 percent of all MCPS high school graduates received a score of 3 or higher (out of a possible 5) on at least one Advanced Placement exam. That percentage is nearly twice the state rate and three times the national rate. (A score of 3 or higher qualifies an entering freshman for college credit in the academic subject covered by the exam.)
- Parent satisfaction ranged from 79.7 percent to 86.7 percent between 2005 and 2010. During the same period, the national average for parent satisfaction remained steady at 54 percent.

Montgomery County's academic achievements continue to improve, despite increases in poverty, population, and students who don't speak English. Weast displays pride that the education gap has narrowed. Amazingly, student achievement across the board has advanced, with low achievers advancing at a rate that's catching the ever-improving high achievers. He refers to a line graph on his iPad, and, as he talks, his finger climbs up the graph: "There's the SAT scores. There's what the nation does, there's what Maryland does, and there's who we are, and we're around 150 points above, on average." For Weast and the Montgomery County Public Schools team, even though the turnaround has been completed, the effort never stops. Through constant striving to learn and a near obsession with innovation, the system keeps advancing.

UNDERSTAND THE CULTURE

Organizations that stay on top have embraced a comprehensive commitment to excellence. As you guide your organization through winning seasons, develop groundbreaking products, and achieve annual growth and more, sustaining success will become a regular focus. In shifting your attention to continual achievement and accepting the sacrifices and efforts that ensure long-standing victory, you will need to turn a more discerning eye to the culture of your team. The culture of your organization is both a reflection and an indication of your team's work ethic, focus, effort, and commitment. This culture will come to define your organization as a tangible representation of who you are and where you're going. Winning cultures don't come easy, but many organizations have found ways to establish and maintain them. Many such organizations exist, but few offer more insight into how to succeed continually than does the NFL's Pittsburgh Steelers organization.

Dan Rooney was inducted into the Pro Football Hall of Fame in 2000 and has served as president or chairman of the Pittsburgh Steelers since 1975. Recently he has taken a more supportive role in the organization, assuming the title of chairman emeritus and focusing on his recent appointment as U.S. Ambassador to Ireland. But not only has Rooney's leadership guided the Pittsburgh franchise for more than three decades, Rooney himself has proved to be one of the most effective leaders ever to emerge through the NFL. In nearly every way, Rooney presents himself as an affable and friendly gentleman. He is modest, soft-spoken, charming, and thoughtful, and he also commands respect. In a sport known for hypermasculine chest-pounders, Rooney has built an empire with his gentle and genuine approach.

The Pittsburgh Steelers are the most successful franchise in the NFL, and the team's relationship with its fans is second to none. Since the merger of the NFL and the AFL, in 1970, no team has been more dominant. From 1970 to 2010, the Steelers have amassed 384 wins against only 246 losses. They've also had twenty division titles, thirty-three postseason wins, eight Super Bowl appearances, and six championship rings.[4] No one's better than the Steelers. In addition to the Steelers' on-field performance, the franchise arguably has the best fans in professional football. In a 2008 ESPN piece that ranked the fans of all NFL teams, those of the Steelers were ranked number one.[5] At the beginning of the 2011 season, the Steelers had sold out every home game, something they had been doing since 1972. Diehard Steelers fans, waving their signature bright yellow "terrible towels," have proved themselves a loyal team behind the team.

In a walk around Steelers headquarters, the mom-and-pop feel of the franchise isn't diminished by the state-of-the-art practice facilities, the fancy plaques, and the memorabilia. The team's colors (black and yellow) adorn the headquarters, and although there is a prominent place for the Steelers' many Vince Lombardi Trophies, awarded for the team's Super Bowl wins, they seem less like a flagrant display of success than like a daily reminder that hard work and continual effort can pay off. In fact, despite the loyal fans, trophies, and achievements, the Steelers franchise seems to operate in a perpetual state of humility. Through a nearly obsessive focus on being familial, kind, and thoughtful, the Rooney family has developed an enduring and unique culture that has become the gold standard for professional sports.

The Pittsburgh Steelers, established in 1933 by Art Rooney, who purchased the squad for a whopping $2,500 (equivalent to $41,600 in 2010), are the fifth oldest franchise in the NFL. Art ran the franchise for more than four decades, but his son Dan was well groomed to assume a leadership role early in his career. Dan has worked in the organization in a variety of capacities since 1955. He assumed substantial leadership duties in the late 1960s and became president in 1975. Also incredibly involved with the development of the NFL at large, Dan is widely considered one of the most respected and dependable owners in the history of the NFL. After nearly thirty years of serving as president of the franchise, in 2002 Dan handed the title of president over to his own son, Art Rooney II, and took on the title of chairman. Dan is the guiding force behind much of the Steelers' success, and he is also the bridge between the organization's founding father and its current president. Dan's insights into the culture of the Steelers are both surprising and genuinely inspiring.

Edgar Schein, professor emeritus at the Sloan School of Management of the Massachusetts Institute of Technology (MIT), suggests that leaders can alter a culture through a variety of efforts, and he breaks culture into three distinct layers: *observable artifacts, values,* and *underlying assumptions.*[6] Observable artifacts are the things that surround you, which you see, hear, touch, taste, or smell. These artifacts are tangible and clear—the team colors, a uniform, smiling team members, and so on. Schein identifies values as a critical element of culture and suggests that they are best identified through conversation but are also reflected in the many artifacts. The values that you subscribe to, believe in, and embrace will be distinct elements of the larger culture you develop. (We explored values in our discussion of stage II of the Team Turnaround Process but are revisiting them here because they are critical to understanding the organization's culture.) These values are palpable and guide the actions of the organization. As for the underlying assumptions of a culture, they are the unique beliefs that support a group's specific values. If a group consistently works after hours, then the underlying assumption may be that working late leads to a competitive edge and to organizational success. Conversely, a company whose employees leave on time and work overtime only when necessary may believe that having interests outside the workplace, such as family, friends, and hobbies, contributes to overall health and wellness and makes for more engaged employees. Neither perspective is wholly correct, but every culture reflects a distinct set of assumptions that explain employees' actions.

In the case of the Steelers, the observable artifacts are everywhere, and they serve as critical reminders of the values and assumptions that the Steelers embrace. In any organization, the paint on the wall, the code of dress, and decorations throughout the office serve as observable artifacts, but the Steelers are obviously different. The attention to detail and the broader messages quickly distinguish them from more average organizations. The prominently positioned trophies, historic memorabilia, and team photos that adorn the offices immediately suggest that the Steelers organization is historic and accomplished. Taking this idea a bit deeper, Rooney suggests that the open office plan represents a conscious effort intended to promote interoffice communication and networking. The more casual style of professional dress and the friendly manner in which people talk with each other are also observable artifacts that craft a distinct environment. Beyond the layout and décor of the franchise's headquarters, the Steelers are rich in artifacts. The team's uniforms, the distinct logo, the players the Steelers draft, the merchandise they sell, the food they serve at the stadium, and the price of their tickets are all artifacts that make up a unique and distinct culture that has proved wildly powerful.

The observable artifacts of the Steelers franchise offer acute insight into the organization's values, but conversation is needed to confirm them. Rooney is pointed in addressing the organization's commitment to specific values, mentioning a variety of principles that range from relationships and honesty to loyalty and integrity. He talks about them with passion and commitment, even providing historical context for some by explaining where the value came from and why it's important. For Rooney, these values are not just things to respect and honor; they're a way of doing business, a key to winning, a guideline for how to live life.

In discussing some of these values, Rooney not only identifies them explicitly but also gives examples of long-standing actions to back them up. Of the organization's commitment to relationships, he explains, "You know, talking to people, and letting them know that you value their opinion, and you have to say okay, well, we don't agree with that, or we do but we've got to pick it up and play it through."[7] Throughout their history, the Steelers have been known as a people-friendly franchise. Rooney is known as a kind and wise man, the organization is committed to keeping tickets affordable for fans, and the very space of the corporate offices has been designed to promote convening, conversation, and good relationships. More specifically, the Steelers gained some press during the 2011 Super Bowl when they were pitted against the Green Bay Packers. Whereas the Packers flew their injured reserves (players who couldn't play because of injuries) on a separate flight, put them up in a different hotel, and excluded them from the team photo, the Steelers treated their injured players as equals. The Steelers flew as a team, injured players and all, stayed in the same hotel, and all appeared in the Super Bowl photo.[8]

Given this commitment to people and relationships, the organization's dedication to loyalty isn't much of a leap. Rooney believes in loyalty, and it runs through the franchise. The

Steelers are famous for their franchisewide support. Previous players are known to show up at championship and playoff games in droves, supporting the current team as interested and dedicated alumni. Perhaps most remarkable is the organization's loyalty to coaches. In an era marked by transition, quick hires and fires, and little patience, the Steelers have hired only three coaches since 1969, a league low. To put that stat into perspective, as of December 2011 the Atlanta Falcons have had fifteen head coaches in the same time frame, several teams have employed fourteen coaches, the Miami Dolphins (who are second in the NFL in wins after 1970) have had eight coaches, and the two teams that trail the Steelers by only one in Super Bowl trophies (the Dallas Cowboys and the San Francisco 49ers) have had twenty-one coaching hires between them.[9] The team closest to matching the Steelers on that stat is the Carolina Panthers, who have hired four coaches, but the Panthers have existed only since 1995. Loyalty runs deep in the Steelers franchise, and, along with the many values the Steelers subscribe to, their commitment is what sets them apart. The Steelers don't just say they're loyal; they stick to loyalty, live by loyalty, and exemplify loyalty.

Artifacts and values are somewhat easy to discern, but the third layer of culture is slightly more difficult to identify. Schein suggests that beneath every value is an underlying assumption that guides stakeholders' actions. An underlying assumption is an unspoken truth within an organization, and it's often not even thought about at a conscious level.[10] It's just there, and it supports the values that exist within the organization. Think back to how the Steelers treated their injured players during the 2011 Super Bowl. Why would a team spend that kind of money on players who weren't going to help on the field? Rooney once said, "We always treated the players as equals. We always treated the players as more than just players. They were family. They were friends."[11] In other words, you don't treat family and friends poorly. Rather, you love them in sickness and in health. You value them and treat them with respect, regardless of the luck that has befallen them. The assumption is that if you're part of the Steelers, you're family, and you'll be treated according to how the organization views family. You'll be treated with compassion and consideration, despite your standing.

Similarly, why would the Steelers remain so loyal to coaches, especially through losing periods? After all, the past thirty years haven't been all good times and smiles. For all the Steelers' successes, there have also been some lean years. Most recently, between 1998 and 2000, Bill Cowher guided the Steelers to a combined record of 22–26, well below .500, and far short of their annual Super Bowl aspirations. The Steelers failed to make the playoffs for those three years, and many organizations would have fired Cowher and looked for a new coach to get the team going, fill the seats, and satisfy restless fans chronically calling for change. But not the Steelers. The underlying assumption behind the Steelers' loyalty is both profound and deeply woven into the history of the organization. To illustrate the assumption behind the Steelers' commitment to loyalty, Rooney recalls a conversation he had with the famed Steelers coach Chuck Noll in the late 1960s. In Noll's first season with Pittsburgh, the Steelers lost 13 out of 14 games, but Rooney remembers Noll explaining that they had to plan for the long run, and that short-term gains wouldn't position the team for long-standing success. For Noll, the race was best won with a consistent and steady commitment to developing talent over time. Games could be won in the short term, but it would be at the expense of larger goals. In order for the Steelers to achieve success in the form of Super Bowl victories, they'd have to be patient and make moves that would help them advance steadily and sustainably.

Noll proved something of a genius, and the franchise ignited. Noll built the famed "steel curtain" defense and is the only NFL coach who has won four Super Bowls, crystalizing the organization's assumption that loyalty leads to success. In spite of the inevitable lows, all three of the Steelers coaches since 1969—Chuck Noll, Bill Cowher, and Mike Tomlin— have Super Bowl rings. What's more, this particular coaching crew has gained nearly unparalleled respect from peers and industry pundits. Both Noll and Cowher were included in Bleacher Report's 2010 piece "NFL Power Rankings: 50 Greatest NFL Head Coaches of All-Time," showing up as number four and number seventeen, respectively, and Tomlin will likely make such lists as he ages into a veteran and a possible Hall of Fame-caliber coach.[12]

Similar to the way in which the Steelers grew to value loyalty, an organization accumulates its underlying assumptions over time. Through the experiences of the larger group, the insights of its leaders, and the collective history that evolves with time, these assumptions become the deepest and most ingrained layer of an organization's culture. In many ways, the Team Turnaround Process is about understanding an underperforming team's assumptions, challenging them, and bringing to light new truths and ways of doing things. Once this occurs, the organization has the opportunity to learn and solidify a new set of assumptions—or, to put it another way, develop a new culture that is more conducive to the larger goals and objectives. In addition, maintaining and managing the assumptions of an organization is necessary to sustaining its success. Organizations like the Pittsburgh Steelers bear this burden with vigilance and pride, ensuring that the underlying assumptions of the franchise are adequate to the franchise's incessant dedication to achievement.

The maintenance of a culture is an ongoing process that requires regular effort.[13] The effort is worthwhile, though, particularly when you take into account just how much culture dictates behavior, focus, ethic, and results. Culture is a powerful component of every organization, and to a certain extent it takes on a life of its own. For the savvy and knowledgeable, however, culture and its components can serve as potent tools. As you gain further insight into the culture that surrounds you, values can be added and removed, artifacts can be built in to further accentuate the desired principles, and assumptions can be further defined and made explicit for your team and your organization. Leadership and culture are intimately woven together, continually impacting and influencing each

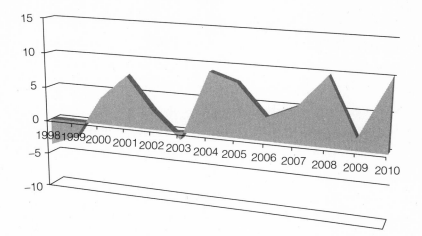

Figure 6.2. SRS for the Pittsburgh Steelers, 1998–2010*
*This figure shows the Simple Rating System (SRS) as it applies to the Pittsburgh Steelers from 1998 through 2010. The SRS, created by sports-reference.com, is a statistical measure of a given team's overall strength, taking into account its margin of victory and the strength of the other teams it is scheduled to play in a given year. The SRS league average is 0. Numbers greater than 0 indicate that a team's performance is stronger than the league average, whereas negative numbers indicate that a team's performance is weaker than the league average.

other. But leadership has a greater impact on culture than culture does on leadership, and as the leader of a team, you are a steward of its culture, an ambassador with the responsibility and power to influence and safeguard a culture of exellence.[14]

As Figure 6.2 shows, the Steelers endured a difficult stretch between 1998 and 2000, but the team's culture was hardly dragging the franchise down. Quite the opposite—the Steelers' long-standing culture of excellence was what kept the franchise advancing through the unavoidable bad times. When the Steelers weather a few bad years, they don't overreact, fire the coach, and yield to fan and media pressure. As Rooney says, "Making changes doesn't help you. All it does is put you back two years. Our belief is, if you're going to change every three years, you're never going to get there."[15] It is because of this belief that the Steelers have remained remarkably steady in terms of ownership, front office personnel, coaches, players, and success. Their culture, "the Steelers Way," is their most powerful asset. The Steelers serve as an example of what can be achieved when an organization embraces and preserves a culture by understanding its assumptions, practicing defined values, and echoing those values through the many artifacts that comprise the organization.

THE PLAYBOOK FOR NURTURING A CULTURE OF EXCELLENCE

Stage VI brings with it a host of challenges that will force you to question how you can continue to improve. To maintain your success, you must focus your efforts on continuing to learn about your organization and your industry, as Jerry Weast did when he focused on taking the Montgomery County Public School System to even greater heights. Pay attention to the details, and dedicate yourself to continuing your education indefinitely. By placing a similar focus on innovation, you will position yourself not only to grow through learning but also to use your knowledge to advance new ideas, new products, and new ways of doing things. Such innovations may not always be profitable, but a dedication to innovation will inevitably lead to processes that push you forward.

As you focus on learning and innovation, pay close attention to your culture. You've turned your team around, but now you want to sustain success. Culture is critical to your long-standing excellence, and values are an integral part of culture. Dan Rooney knows this and has instilled strong values in the Pittsburgh Steelers, values that are reflected throughout the franchise's history, facilities, and team. All of this comprises a culture of excellence that continues to drive the organization to unparalleled success on and off the football field. Your culture is your organization. By monitoring it, preserving it, and caring for it, you can establish a commitment to achievement that lasts well into the future.

Commit your organization to excellence and long-term success. Don't take your achievements up to this point for granted. Keep doing what you've done to get here. Continue to learn, dedicate yourself to innovation, and take time both to understand and further define a culture that will drive success for years to come. There are going to be dips in the road. Things are not always going to run smoothly. But if you establish a culture for sustained success, your organization will continue to excel.

The Team
Turnaround
Workbook

Through the Team Turnaround Process, your organization can transform itself from a poorly performing group at stage I to a team that adopts a culture of sustained excellence at stage VI. The Team Turnaround Process is presented as a neat, organized, six-stage model, but reality is never quite this clean. Not only will your turnaround journey be different from the stories in this book, your personnel, industry, and goals will present distinct challenges. The exercises in this chapter will assist you on your path and help you and your team work through the Team Turnaround Process.

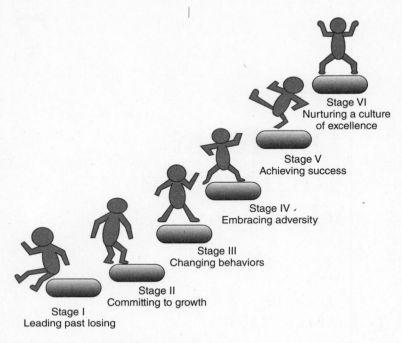

Stage VI
Nurturing a culture
of excellence

Stage V
Achieving success

Stage IV
Embracing adversity

Stage III
Changing behaviors

Stage II
Committing to growth

Stage I
Leading past losing

The Team Turnaround Process

This chapter is intended to help you guide your group forward, so take some time to think about what stage of the Team Turnaround Process you and your team are in. Some exercises are labeled "Leader's Worksheet" and are intended solely for the team leader. Others, labeled "Group Exercise," are intended for the leader to use with the larger team. Exercises that might benefit from having a more objective outside facilitator are labeled with the letter F in parentheses (F). In large part, these activities are reflection- and discussion-based because no turnaround can occur without open, honest, and consistent communication.

Good luck as you embark on the Team Turnaround Process!

STAGE I: LEADING PAST LOSING

The following statements are true of teams at stage I:

- They are losing, and oftentimes they are losing big.
- They have no clear performance goals; or, if they do have appropriate performance goals, those goals are not being met.
- They are not being held accountable for their failures.
- They may not believe that there is a better way of doing things, and they are unaware of how to move the group forward.
- They deny or rationalize away the severity of the problems they are facing.
- They lack open and honest communication, and what communication they do have is otherwise faulty as well.
- They have roles and expectations that are ambiguous and/ or poorly matched with the team members' skills.

At this stage, the leader has the following responsibilities:

- To explore the reasons for poor performance
- To reflect on what the team could be
- To discern whether team members' stated causes for failure are actual causes or simply rationalizations

- To tell team members the truth about the reasons for their poor performance
- To learn how other leaders have inspired success in similar situations

When you first join an underperforming team or realize that your group is in the throes of stage I, your knee-jerk response may be to act. As counterintuitive as this may seem, however, action needs to wait. Rushing to do something is analogous to a doctor's prescribing a knee brace for a patient complaining of knee pain. The brace might alleviate the immediate problem, but what if the structure of the knee is damaged and a ligament is torn? What if the issue is really misalignment of the hip, or an abnormal gait, or lack of blood flow to the knee? By acting prematurely, the doctor loses a critical opportunity to separate the symptom from the core problem(s) and may actually exacerbate the issue.

Quick action is unlikely to lead to long-term sustainable performance. Jeffrey Lurie of the Philadelphia Eagles, Frank Esposito of Kendon Industries, and David Helfer of Juniper Networks all understood this and painstakingly gathered information before they took action. Lurie, Esposito, and Helfer first studied and worked to understand the core issues that were plaguing their teams, where improvements were needed, and what was going wrong. If you want to build for long-term, sustainable performance, you're going to have put the time in up front to better understand your team's processes, composition, interactions, alignment, and strategy. Only after

understanding how the team works can you possibly understand what is wrong and what needs to be fixed.

In order to analyze your team effectively, you may need
to question some of the basic assumptions of the team's very
existence. The following pages contain several exercises and
questions you can use to guide your exploration. By taking the
time to understand why your team is failing, you will prepare
yourself to lead the team forward.

Observe and Learn: Leader's Worksheet

In beginning this exploratory process, the primary question is
obviously "Why are we losing?" In order to understand this issue
more fully, you need to examine the team, its expectations, how
it is failing, and where problems are occurring.

1. When Jeffrey Lurie purchased the Philadelphia Eagles, he
    knew they weren't performing on the field, but he didn't
    understand how deeply they were failing as an organization.
    He took time to discover, through intense observation,
    where the organization was losing. Spend some time observ-
    ing your own team, and answer the following questions:
    - What is your team failing to achieve?
    - What needs to be fixed?
2. In order for team members to effectively carry out their
    roles, it's critical that they have the necessary tools. To
    determine whether or not your team members have what

they need to get the job done, ask yourself the following questions:

- What skills necessary for the job do individual team members lack?
- What can you do to help them acquire those skills?

3. Most underperforming teams have members who display behaviors that do not contribute to the cohesiveness or productivity of the group, but those behaviors are tolerated because "that's the way things have always been." The Eagles' equipment manager refused to give equipment to the players, and his actions had a direct, negative effect on the players' performance and satisfaction. Take a look at your team, and ask yourself these questions to identify and address negative behaviors they may be displaying or battling:

- What specific behaviors impede the group or harm interpersonal relations?
- What important behaviors are absent that could help the group?

4. David Helfer analyzed his team at Juniper Networks to better understand roles, expectations, and how talent could be matched with tasks. As you begin to analyze your team, ask yourself these questions to help yourself consider how your team functions and whether roles will need to be further assessed:

- Who does what?
- Are the right people in position to get the job done?

- Could the team function more effectively if roles were defined differently?

Observe and Learn: Group Exercise

Note to the leader: Use your best judgment on whether to conduct this exercise in a group setting or through individual conversations with group members.

Frank Esposito asked every member of his team at Kendon Industries the following three questions to better understand where and how they were failing:

- If you were in my role, what are three things that you would change?
- What are we doing that's stupid?
- What do you think our customers think about this team?

By asking the questions in the two preceding exercises, you will gain valuable insights related to your team members and the issues that have held them back. As tempting as it will be to take action once the information begins to come in, it's important to refrain from acting. You're building a foundation, and these initial questions are just breaking ground. Supplement the answers you get with more intense inquiry, interviews, and any quantifiable performance metrics you can find (for example, metrics related to sales, wins, goals, earnings, and so on). As you gather more information, you will be able to construct a comprehensive narrative about how and why your team has sunk to its current level. Only when you have reached that point should you take your findings to the team, addressing team members with the facts and sharing the truths you've uncovered.

Face Reality: Leader's Worksheet

After you have had time to observe the workings of your team, you will no doubt have uncovered some ugly truths about the group's performance. At this point, it is necessary for you to communicate these truths to the group. It is critical for group members to understand and respond to the truth so they can stop denying, justifying, and rationalizing their underwhelming performance. As the leader, you must be the truth teller and challenge the team with the reality that it is underperforming but doesn't have to. Consider the following questions:

1. How is the team rationalizing and/or denying its poor performance?
2. What will happen if team members continue to deny and/ or rationalize their poor performance? What are the consequences?
3. What needs to happen for poor performance to change?
4. How can this message be delivered so the group will hear and understand it?

By considering these questions before you challenge the team, you will position yourself to construct a logical and emotionally appealing argument for change.

Face Reality: Group Activity (F)

Now that you have announced the performance issues that you think are plaguing the team, it's also important for the team to acknowledge them. While it's necessary for team members to hear these truths from you, it can be helpful if they are engaged in the process of further exploring them. One way to gain additional insight and buy-in regarding the performance concerns debilitating a team is through the exercise of creating a fishbone diagram, a tool developed by Kaoru Ishikawa in the 1960s to illuminate root causes of specific problems.[1] This exercise can include all the members of a team, and it is an excellent way to distinguish symptoms from root causes while inviting the multiple perspectives of the group.

- To start the fishbone diagram, the facilitator writes down a clear problem statement—for example, "Team falling short of overall performance by 20 percent." This statement, which can reflect one of the ugly truths uncovered through the previous worksheet, is called the *effect statement.* Once the group agrees on the statement, draw a box around the statement to represent the head of the fish, and then draw a line trailing from the head to serve as the spine. In the following illustration, the effect statement is simply "Low attendance at games."

[1] K. Ishikawa, *Introduction to Quality Control* (New York: Productivity Press, 1990).

- Next, broader *cause categories* are drawn, serving as ribs extending from the spine. Cause categories are general areas from which problems might originate. For example, cause categories used in the service industry might take the form of the eight P's (product, price, place, promotion, people, process, physical evidence, and productivity), whereas a manufacturing team might employ the eight M's (machine, method, material, manpower, measurement, management, maintenance, and Mother Nature/environment). Regardless of the categories you use, each broader cause category needs to relate back to the effect statement. The following illustration shows the initial effect statement, along with the cause categories branching from the spine.

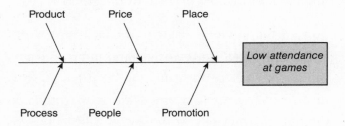

- For each cause category, a general question related to how the cause category impacts the problem should be posed. For example, "How does price [the cause category] contribute to this problem?" As ideas are provided by the team, the facilitator notes each one as a "bone" from the appropriate cause category. It's possible for these subcauses to be placed in more than one cause category. To create the following illustration, the facilitator connected numerous bones to the "Product" cause category because the team believed that the product was substantially related to the original effect statement.

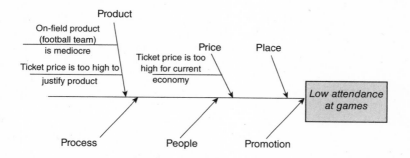

- With each idea, a good facilitator will probe responses by asking "Why?" Pushing yourselves to find a deeper meaning in the responses will ensure that the exercise produces valued results. Asking "Why?" can guide the deeper inquiry and reflection that are critical for forward movement. Here is the completed fishbone diagram.

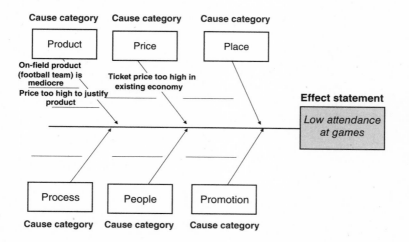

After all the cause categories have been discussed, review your findings with the team. Make sure that the entire group has clarity on what contributes to the problem. Ideally, your team will leave the exercise with a richer understanding of group issues and of why they exist. In addition to using the fishbone diagram to identify problems to solve, you can revisit the results when old rationalizations and denial resurface.

Define Roles and Responsibilities: Leader's Worksheet

When David Helfer of Juniper Networks began working with his current team, he simply asked team members what their jobs were. From this simple question, Helfer gained a better understanding of his employees' perceptions of their roles and what they thought they were being judged by. At times he was surprised by the responses because they were far from accurate, but each conversation gave him an opportunity to reinforce the employee's actual role and specific expectations and to determine whether the employee was the right fit for the job function. The following questions will help you engage in a dialogue to better understand the roles and expectations of your team members:

1. What is each individual's role?
2. What are your expectations of each individual?

3. If a member falls short of your expectations, what can he or she expect?

4. If you are not meeting a team member's expectations, how should he or she approach you?

5. How can you ensure that each team member understands his or her role?

6. How can you continually communicate your expectations to the team? What channels will you use?

The answers to these questions will help you gain clarity regarding what your team members think they should be doing and what you expect of them. With this information, you can begin to communicate precise roles, responsibilities, and expectations to employees. In addition, you can determine whether any employees are ill suited to their current roles and identify more appropriate ones. A conversation about roles and responsibilities can clarify any role ambiguity and help team members move forward with the confidence that their efforts are aligned with their roles and your expectations.

STAGE II: COMMITTING TO GROWTH

The following statements are true of teams at stage II:

- They fully recognize that they are not performing adequately.
- They feel an intense drive to be better.

- They are ready to strive for larger achievements, even if those now seem vague and somewhat unattainable.
- They need more specific plans composed of goals and values.
- They are excited to begin a new journey.

At this stage, the leader has the following responsibilities:

- To develop and communicate a vision
- To identify and articulate the values that will guide the group forward, providing team members necessary direction regarding how they will go about achieving their vision and goals
- To develop the larger plan and smaller goals

In stage II, your team members should have a better understanding of what is expected of them and of what they can expect from the organization. Whereas stage I is largely about identifying and accepting where the team is in the present, stage II is about accepting the reality of poor performance and about planning for the future. At this stage, you will begin to plan where the group will go and how you'll guide it there. Specifically, the focus in stage II is on vision, values, and corresponding goals, and your efforts will be concentrated on inspiring the group to move forward. Stage II is defined by hope—the idea that the group can and will get better.

Launch the Vision: Leader's Worksheet

The manner in which a vision is developed and communicated can make or break its success. Bill Polian, onetime president of the Indianapolis Colts, walked into a failing organization and declared his vision for the team—a Super Bowl championship. Given that every vision is both personal to the leader and unique to the team being led, what will your vision be? The vision must serve as a beacon to guide the team toward greater success. It has to resonate at a deep level and excite team members about the upcoming journey. Your vision can be a very powerful tool for rallying the troops, and so it is crucial that you take the time to develop a compelling and inspiring vision. Ask yourself the following questions:

1. What are you and the team capable of when you're performing at your best?
2. What has the team accomplished in the past that suggests greatness moving forward?
3. What existing thoughts, achievements, or team concepts can you incorporate into your vision?
4. What is your vision for this team? Remember that an effective vision is short, is concrete, and reflects who you are as a person and as a leader.
5. How can you communicate your vision, both initially and on a consistent basis? It is important that you consider how the vision can be communicated through words as well as actions.

This exercise serves three purposes. First, it will help you construct a portrait of what the team could look like and what it could accomplish. Second, it will help you make the changes easier for the group as you consider who the team is and how team members can draw on their past to move forward. Third, it will help you develop a communication strategy so you can deliver your vision more clearly and comprehensively.

Launch the Vision: Group Exercise

In order to get the rest of the team involved in the vision-forming process, you can make creating a vision into an engaging exercise.

- Split the team into groups of four to five people.
- Ask the subgroups a simple question: "What would you want a respected publication [for example, *Harvard Business Review* or *Fast Company* or whatever is most relevant to your industry] to write about this team in seven years?"
- Task each group with developing a bulleted list on a flip chart that captures what the members think they are capable of, what others will recognize in them, and what they will work toward during the seven-year time period.
- After about twenty to forty minutes, have each individual group present its response to the rest of the team.

- During the presentations, highlight and discuss group responses that reach toward the future, that include creative ideas about what the group can achieve, and that offer specific direction regarding where the group should strive to go.

By engaging the group in the vision process, you gain valuable insight into what team members want to become. Incorporate this information into the larger vision, and let them know that what they think matters. This exercise also provides an opportunity to see what limits the team is placing on its own potential. Chances are that you may need to convince team members to reach farther than they think they can.

Adopt Guiding Values: Group Exercise #1

Values provide a framework for what's important and help reduce anxiety by answering questions regarding how people should act as they strive for their visions and goals. Values are a critical component of any organization's culture, and ultimately they guide the behavior of the larger group. Jim Grundberg of SeeMore Putters identified his company's guiding values as customer service and technology. Recall how SeeMore Putters demonstrated those values through what the company said and did. To do this in your organization, it is important to consider what your team's values are and to plan for how those values can be implemented and consistently acted out.

1. Ask one simple question that focuses team members on the values they were living out while they were underperforming—for example, "What were the values that you exhibited last year, and how did they contribute to your performance?"
2. Compare and contrast the values of the team when it was losing to the values of a winning team.

This simple exercise will provide you with insight into what team members valued when they were losing. It will also help you identify what the group needs to value in order to win.

Adopt Guiding Values: Group Exercise #2 (F)

This exercise will allow you to explore group values and, in the process, help you gain keen insight into the various perceptions of each team member. It will also provide you with a solid foundation on which to establish clear behaviors and expectations for living out the values that are ultimately recognized and formally adopted by the team.

1. Without prior discussion, have each team member write down the three core values he or she believes the team must have to achieve its vision.

2. Once the team has come together as a group, have each team member write down, on a shared whiteboard or poster board, the values that he or she came up with.

3. Through group discussion, examine these values on three different levels:

   ■ *Surface:* Discuss what's on the board, the facts that lie in front of you, the commonalities, and the outliers. Have team members who advocated for less popular values explain their reasoning. Similarly, have group members discuss the more common values: Why did they continue to come up? How might they help the larger team?

   ■ *Internal:* Discuss how the values might work to help internal interactions within the team. In other words, have team members outline how the values might provide a framework in which to operate internally.

   ■ *External:* Discuss how the values on the board might assist with relations outside the group, and how they might impact external business dynamics.

4. Take special note of the values that continue to surface during the conversation, and of the values that seem to have been left behind.

5. Now have the group as a whole select three to five values, based on the discussion, that seem to resonate with the larger team and to align with the larger vision. Work to ensure that everyone's voice, including your own, is heard, and that less vocal members of the team have an opportunity to express their opinions.

6. Now discuss what types of day-to-day actions and behaviors represent each value, and determine what the group can do to live out the values that have been identified.

Through this exercise, you will not only define clear values that the group can subscribe to but also identify critical actions that will assist team members in living out the values that resonate with them.

Establish a Plan: Group Exercise (F)

Just as Jere Harris and his colleagues determined a plan for how *Spider-Man: Turn Off the Dark* would eventually open as a successful Broadway show, you will need to develop a plan that will guide your team forward. To develop your plan, you can use the *critical success factor* (CSF) format, which identifies the factors that are critical to your team's success.[1] CSFs are the essential areas that, if addressed appropriately, will ensure that your team competes successfully. Jere Harris believed that the *Spider-Man* team had three CSFs: to understand what the audience wanted, to change the storyline to reflect the audience's desires, and to relaunch the new product.

[1] J. F. Rockart, "Chief Executives Define Their Own Data Needs," *Harvard Business Review* 57:2 (1979), 81–93.

1. To identify your team's CSFs, simply ask the team, "What are the critical success factors, or essential areas we need to address, for our team to succeed?"

2. Now that you have identified your CSFs, how can they be prioritized to form the framework of a plan?

These questions will provide valuable insight into what the group considers critical to achieving its vision. This exercise may seem simple, but the conversation it generates will be powerful and valuable. Be prepared for intense discussion because there will be differing perspectives about what is critical and what can be ignored. Some team members may fight to justify their contributions, and they may become steadfast in protecting their places in the shop. Listen for arguments that become more selfish, and be prepared to redirect the group toward focusing on what is critical for the team's long-term achievement.

Develop Goals: Group Exercise

Now that you have identified the factors that will be critical to your success, you will have plenty of fodder for developing clear goals. Some of the CSFs you've identified may actually serve as goals, whereas others will not. For example, a soccer team may consider soccer balls and daily practice critical to its success, but obtaining soccer balls may be irrelevant as a goal, whereas daily practice could prove to be a goal worth making explicit. Review the CSFs you've identified as a group, and determine the goals you will need to achieve in order to advance toward the larger vision. Consider the following questions as you brainstorm:

1. What do we need to accomplish as we work toward each CSF?
2. What do we need to achieve every day in order to believe that we are successfully making progress toward the CSFs?
3. What extra efforts are necessary in order to achieve each CSF?

By developing a list of possible goals, you will outline exactly what types of things need to happen in order for you to continually progress. Your list will likely need further refinement, but at least you and the team are sharing the belief that specific things need to be achieved in order for the larger vision to be accomplished.

SMART Goals: Group Exercise

Once the list of goals has been developed, it can be helpful to discuss each one in the context of the SMART goal framework (the acronym stands for goals that are *s*pecific, *m*easurable, *a*ttainable, *r*elevant, and *t*ime-sensitive).

Specific	• What is the goal? • Who is involved? • What does it pertain to?
Measurable	• Are metrics in place to measure progress? • If not, can metrics be created? • How (and by whom) will progress be measured?
Attainable	• Is this goal achievable with the resources available? • If we need additional resources, what are they?
Relevant	• How does this goal connect with our ultimate objective? • Is it truly related to our critical success factors?
Time-sensitive	• By when does this goal need to be completed?

By making your goals compliant with the SMART goal framework, you will create a list of goals that are actionable. Make sure that by the time you finish this exercise, you have actionable goals and clear instructions regarding who will do what, by when. After all, these are the issues that the entire team needs to focus on and must have clarity around in order for the team to accomplish its larger vision.

STAGE III: CHANGING BEHAVIORS

The following statements are true of teams at stage III:

■ They consciously strive to change.
■ They focus on the small behaviors and actions that lead to success.

- Team members trust each other for encouragement and correction as the group strives to break bad habits and adopt new, more productive ones.

At this stage, the leader has the following responsibilities:

- To educate the team about the behaviors and actions needed for success
- To model appropriate behaviors and rely on key personnel to do the same
- To address old, inappropriate behaviors when they reappear, and to continually reinforce the behaviors needed for success
- To identify and manufacture successes so that team members feel the progress they are making
- To celebrate successes explicitly and joyfully

Up to this point, you and your team have been inwardly focused on what you have become, on what you want to be, on where you want to go, and on how you plan to get there. You have helped your team increase its awareness and develop a plan that, if executed, can lead to success. At stage III, you move from planning and introspection to execution. When you execute your plan, there will be setbacks, but it is the role of the leader not only to model and encourage the behaviors that lead to success but also to identify and correct the behaviors that will inevitably carry over from the earlier days of losing.

Understanding the Stages of Change: Leader's Worksheet

James Prochaska, John Norcross, and Carlo DiClemente developed the transtheoretical model of behavior change. In the model outlined by these three researchers, individuals progress from *precontemplation* to *contemplation* to *preparation,* and finally they advance from *action* to *maintenance.* According to this model, people slowly move from ignoring their problem behaviors to acknowledging and learning about the negative impact of their actions, and then to changing. Throughout this process, different tools are critical for continued progress. Understanding where employees are in the behavior-change process can assist you in meeting them with the appropriate interventions. The following figure illustrates the stages of an individual's behavior-change progress.

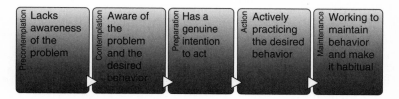

Transtheoretical Model
Source: Adapted from J. O. Prochaska, J. C. Norcross, and C. C. DiClemente, *Changing for Good* (New York: Avon, 1994).

Teach What's Right: Leader's Worksheet

When Ani Shabazian (Chapter Four) explained to an employee that listening to an iPod at work was inappropriate, she was bringing that employee from *precontemplation* (not even considering the action as inappropriate) to *contemplation* (thinking about the implications and impact of the action). As you become familiar with the transtheoretical model of change, you can make an educated guess about which stage of behavior change an employee might be in. Once you believe you have identified where an individual falls in the behavior-change process, you can target the appropriate type of intervention using the following table. Instead of simply telling the employee to change, you can use the table to guide him or her toward more purposeful action. If you align your actions as a leader with the stage the employee is in, you can be more effective when working with that employee to change his or her behavior.

Stage	Management Goal	Management Intervention
Precontemplation	Increase the employee's awareness of a specific problem behavior or of the need for a more effective behavior	• Provide education • Conduct an individual conversation • Explain how the behavior impacts performance • Explain how the behavior impacts the team
Contemplation	Help the employee to consider his or her behavior and why change may be necessary	• Assist with evaluation of the pros and cons of behavior change • Outline expected outcomes if behavior does change
Preparation	Encourage preparation by gently nudging the employee toward action and increasing the feeling of support	• Work with the employee to define and overcome obstacles • Encourage small first steps • Assist with the planning that goes into making a change
Action	Encourage and support the employee, and celebrate his or her successes	• Ensure that the employee has appropriate support • Celebrate new outcomes
Maintenance	Help to reinforce and refine needed and successful behaviors	• Reinforce behaviors that lead to success through explicit mention and celebration • Offer advice for and guidance toward the continual refinement of behaviors

Model What's Right: Leader's Worksheet

One of the major reasons why Marilyn Masaitis is so effective in leading Marilyn's Cafe is that her actions consistently model the behaviors that she expects her employees to display. As the leader, your actions can go a long way toward further ingraining desired and successful behaviors in your team. Conversely, if your actions are inconsistent with your words, confusion and frustration will likely take root among team members. Nothing will destroy a team's willingness to change faster than the possibility that you are not walking the talk. At the end of each workday, take five minutes to reflect on your actions and ask yourself the following questions:

1. What did I do today to serve as a role model for the group? What did I model?
2. Were there any crises that occurred today? If so, how did I address them, and were my efforts effective?
3. Did I do anything today that may have undermined the team's success?
4. How can I continue to set a standard for the team with my actions?

This simple act of self-reflection can promote deepened awareness about what you're doing to lead your team to success.

The exercise is not intended to be wholly positive. Leaders will make mistakes, and this exercise will help you identify yours. If you've undermined the success of the team, then work to remedy your mistake quickly and decisively. Similarly, if you struggle to come up with day-to-day actions that are supporting and advancing the efforts of the team, it may help to identify new efforts that you can integrate into your routine. We can all improve, and pushing yourself to be the best leader you can be will not only position you to lead effectively but also inspire and guide your team forward.

Reinforce What's Right: Leader's Worksheet

Because most leaders are achievement-oriented, your thoughts may likely be dominated by the question of what's next. If you're always looking ahead, however, you will miss opportunities to celebrate the small accomplishments and successes that your team achieves along the way. Stopping to celebrate is as essential as holding team members accountable when they miss the mark. Your focus may naturally gravitate toward accountability, but celebrations of success are needed for continued growth. Most basketball coaches wouldn't celebrate their eighth win of the season, but Kim Mulkey did because she knew it represented progress. A celebration can be as simple as a pat on the back, public recognition through a group e-mail, or praise during a private meeting, but the key is to acknowledge success in some manner. By asking the following two simple questions at some point during every day, you can raise your awareness of when successes occur and of how you're celebrating them:

1. What occurred today to demonstrate that an individual or the team is making progress?
2. How can I recognize these accomplishments?

Because it is critical as well to hold team members accountable to the standards that have been set, also ask yourself these questions every day:

1. What setbacks occurred today that could compromise the progress of the team?
2. Were these setbacks addressed? If not, how can team members be held accountable to prevent similar setbacks in the future?

Once you raise your awareness of your team's successes and setbacks, take appropriate action. Go visit with your team members and acknowledge their progress, or their difficulties. Either way, let them know that you've noticed, that you care, and that you're committed to their progress.

STAGE IV: EMBRACING ADVERSITY

The following statements are true of teams at stage IV:

- They embrace the opportunity to accept setbacks and challenges.
- They experience the excitement of new challenges, new concerns, and new successes.

- They embrace the opportunity to prove themselves on a bigger stage.
- They take on new sets of obstacles that will spark development and growth.
- They gain the confidence and belief that come with successfully overcoming larger setbacks.

At this stage, the leader has the following responsibilities:

- To appropriately frame obstacles as challenges that will allow for growth
- To embrace and sometimes even create larger crises for team members to rally around
- To promote and develop resilience in the team

As teams begin to win, they inevitably meet with obstacles and challenges. In spite of these barriers, the most successful teams embrace challenges, considering these to be a means of bonding, improving, and moving forward. At stage IV, you must learn to see challenges as opportunities because in doing so you will guide your team to continued success.

Embrace Challenges: Leader's Worksheet

As you encourage team members to embrace challenges, help them by identifying what needs to change, what will happen to the group if the change efforts are unsuccessful, and how the change aligns with the team's long-term success. The following table will help guide you through the exercise of identifying challenges and how best to deal with them. Just as Domino's Pizza grew by embracing multiple challenges, use these challenges as rallying cries for continued effort and success.

Step	Description	Guiding Questions
1	Identify challenges	• What could conceivably occur that would derail the team's efforts? • What is a priority?
2	Set a deadline	• When will this obstacle impact us, and when do we need to deal with it?
3	Identify consequences	• What are the repercussions if we do not deal with the challenge? • What will happen to the larger group? • How will the team's success be impacted?
4	Identify who is impacted and how	• What will happen to the team if the challenge is not embraced? • What will happen to the team's constituents if the challenge is ignored?
5	Identify benefits	• If the challenge is overcome, how will that help the team in the short term? • How will overcoming the challenge benefit the team moving forward?
6	Deliver the message	• How can the message of embracing the challenge be delivered quickly and concisely? • Through what media can the message be delivered?

Once you have identified a challenge to embrace and have established a message that will call your team to arms, it's important that you relentlessly focus your efforts on overcoming the obstacle. This challenge is a unifying opportunity for your team to prove itself. Go out and tackle the challenge, and prove that you're getting better, more powerful, and more competent at overcoming setbacks.

Embrace Challenges: Group Exercise

Domino's Pizza embraced a variety of challenges related to customer satisfaction, public relations, and product quality. All these obstacles were seen by Domino's as opportunities to improve while proving competent and capable. Learning to see challenges as opportunities to prove your stuff can be a powerful and motivating exercise. The following questions will help team members learn to think positively about the challenges they face:

1. What problems are we currently facing that can be viewed as challenges to embrace?
2. How can current problems help us grow as a team?
3. How can current problems be confronted so as to showcase our abilities and potential?

When you embrace challenges as a means to see just how good your team is, what once seemed overwhelming may come to seem manageable and exciting.

Build Resilience: Group Exercise (F)

Building a resilient team is critical to long-term success. A team needs to be able to take on challenges without disintegrating as soon as things become difficult. Resilience is a term that encapsulates a range of concepts, including positive thinking, flexible thinking, problem solving, and gratitude. Resilience is a mind-set that is developed through practice, experience, and reflection. Where Bill Stoneman of the Los Angeles Angels saw a market that had millions of people, hundreds of businesses, and immense potential, his predecessors had seen a small-market club that could never compete with the large-market teams. In many ways, we have a lot of leeway in terms of how we perceive the world. Unfortunately, once we make our decision on whether something is good or bad, our perceptions solidify, and we begin to look for evidence that only reinforces our opinions. In challenging your team to find evidence that supports more positive conclusions and perspectives, you can drive home the concept that our perceptions are influenced by our choices.

- Ask your team to identify two or three things that are widely perceived as negative (either within or external to your team). These can range from a lack of resources to external market factors that may be impacting progress.
- Ensure that there is consensus, or near consensus, with the final discussion points.

- Once the group has agreed on two or three negative issues, have team members brainstorm with one another about how each of these negatives can be perceived as a positive.
- Encourage your team to put genuine effort into working through this exercise, and take time to identify realistic alternatives to the initial negative perceptions.

Upon completion of the exercise, the facilitator can drive home the key point that perception drives perspective. We choose to view the world, our team, challenges, and progress as positive or negative, and we can modify our perspective by adjusting our perceptions. We can look at the same issue in two very different ways, and perhaps we often should. Resilience is strengthened with positivity, and taking the time to look on the bright side will actually enhance your team's ability to take on and work through challenges.

A Problem-Solving Model: Group Exercise

This exercise is based on a six-step problem-solving process developed by Edgar Schein, formerly of the MIT Sloan School of Management.[1] The exercise is intended to help you identify, define, and generate potential solutions to problems.

[1] Edgar H. Schein, *Process Consultation Revisited: Building the Helping Relationship*, 1st ed. (Reading, Mass.: Addison-Wesley, 1999).

Schein's model breaks the problem-solving process into two cycles of activity, each consisting of three steps. Cycle 1 encompasses the steps taken before a decision or an action has been chosen, and cycle 2 encompasses the steps taken after the decision or action has been chosen.

This exercise is best conducted with plenty of time for discussion, and the objective is for the group to work through and become comfortable with the process of identifying and resolving a specific challenge. This process can take a lot of time, so take breaks and/or schedule multiple meetings when necessary, but have confidence that time is not being wasted and that the needed progress is being made.

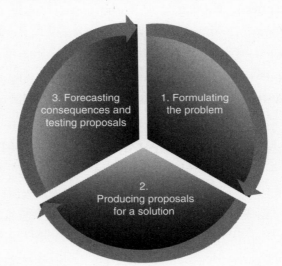

Schein Problem-Solving Process, Cycle 1
Source: Adapted from Edgar H. Schein, *Process Consultation Revisited: Building the Helping Relationship,* 1st ed. (Reading, Mass.: Addison-Wesley, 1999). Used by permission of Pearson Education, Inc., Upper Saddle River, N.J.

Cycle 1

1. *Formulating the problem:* The objective of this step is to clearly identify the problem. Teams get into trouble when they come up with solutions for *symptoms* rather than solutions for *core problems,* and so it is critical to correctly identify and define the core problem. The problem may very well have multiple root causes, but the following questions will help you narrow in on the true concern:

   ■ What is occurring that is problematic?

   ■ Whom/what does it involve?

   ■ How is it impacting us?

   ■ Is it a symptom of a deeper issue, or is it a core concern?

2. *Producing proposals for a solution:* Now it is time to generate solutions. The best way to do this is to brainstorm openly by accepting all ideas and by refraining from judgment and personal attachment to any one suggestion.

   ■ Write down any and all ideas, without discussing or judging their value or even their plausibility.

   ■ Once all ideas have been recorded, go back and evaluate the resulting list by eliminating solutions that are obviously untenable and circling those ideas that are particularly plausible, that are attractive to the group, or that have commonalities with other solutions.

   ■ Compile a list of multiple solutions that may adequately address the initial problem.

3. *Forecasting consequences and testing proposals:* The final step of cycle 1 is to attempt to predict the consequences of implementing the solutions you've identified.

- Have the team visualize the implementation of each solution, step by step, and what the consequences of its implementation might be.
- Have the team identify potential unintended consequences that could evolve into problems down the road.
- Have the group assess which of the solutions will work best and commit to its implementation.

Cycle 1 is complete when the group makes a decision regarding a final solution. This may be a natural point in the process for the team to take a break, but you need to emphasize that the job is not complete. Yes, a solution and its potential impact have been defined, but the solution now needs to be implemented. For this reason, cycle 2 of Schein's problem-solving model starts with action planning.

Cycle 2

4. *Planning actions:* You now need to guide the group in the development of an action plan that includes accountability and responsibilities assigned to specific members—in other words, who needs to do what, and by when? By the end of this step, the team should have clear tasks and deadlines as well as a scheduled time to meet and discuss further progress. The following questions will help the team identify roles and responsibilities:

- What needs to be done to implement the solution?
- What roles need to be filled?
- How will those roles interact?

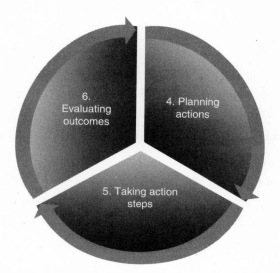

Schein Problem-Solving Process, Cycle 2
Source: Adapted from Edgar H. Schein, *Process Consultation Revisited: Building the Helping Relationship,* 1st ed. (Reading, Mass.: Addison-Wesley, 1999). Used by permission of Pearson Education, Inc., Upper Saddle River, N.J.

5. *Taking action steps:* Individual team members now need to execute their responsibilities. It can be helpful to reconvene at different points in the implementation process to ensure that the necessary actions are being taken, that deadlines are being met, and that communication between team members continues to be effective.

6. *Evaluating outcomes:* Once the project has been completed, you will need to evaluate your efforts. The evaluation process is critical to long-term success, and you must be prepared to go back to the first step of cycle I if the problem

persists. Here are questions that can guide the evaluation process:

- Was the action plan effectively carried out?
- Did the action plan lead to the intended outcomes while addressing the initial problem?
- Have there been any unintended consequences?

Using this type of structure, your team repeatedly has the opportunity to face down its challenges by developing and executing solutions. In repeatedly going through this process, your team will develop collective confidence from the mounting belief that it can overcome any challenge it faces. Through this process, your team will actually be developing its resilience.

STAGE V: ACHIEVING SUCCESS

The following statements are true of teams at stage V:

- They develop a profound and deserved sense of self-satisfaction.
- They experience a sense of confidence, or sincere belief that anything is achievable.
- They experience tangible, outward success.
- They are concerned about how to move on to the next challenge, and about what the next challenge should be.
- They make the effort to develop new goals, adapt, and maintain an edge.

At this stage, the leader has the following responsibilities:

- To increase the awareness within the team of how it judges success
- To continually look to the horizon to find new challenges, goals, and obstacles
- To maintain awareness of the external and internal environment and consciously strive to adapt

By stage V, your team has actualized its potential, made it to the big game, and proved that it's a legitimate contender. As you have racked up multiple victories, however, you have also developed a personal and unique definition of success, one that has evolved over time. By defining what success means to you, and by being open to adapting, you will guide your team to unprecedented levels of achievement.

My Definition of Success: Leader's Worksheet

At this point in its development, your team has already achieved success at a high level. Nevertheless, it's still your responsibility to develop and articulate new challenges, new ways to measure growth, and a new standard of achievement. Take time out of your schedule on a monthly basis to reflect on the following questions:

1. What is our definition of success moving forward?
2. Why is this definition critical, and how does it differ from previous definitions?

Once you decide on a definition you feel comfortable with, you need to determine whether you want to share it with your team, and how you will clearly articulate this new theme. This could prove to be more of an individual exercise, one that will push you as the leader to continually reach toward a higher ideal. If you choose to share your definition, however, it's important to explain why this personal definition of success is meaningful to you, and how it can positively impact the entire team.

Define Success: Group Exercise

Even if you have an individual definition for success, it's important to understand your team's definition. In order to learn how your team defines success, you need to ask. Use the following two questions to guide individual reflection as well as group discussion about what success means to team members and to the larger group:

1. How do we currently define success?
   Consider the following additional questions to advance the conversation:
   - Is success something that is measured in relation to competing organizations, or is it measured in relation to our own performance?
   - Is success a specific goal? Does our team focus on elements of performance that can be controlled (such as effort, or number of calls made per day) or on concepts

that cannot be controlled (such as the idea of outperforming our competitors)?

2. How should we define success?
   - What does this definition say about us? about our goals? about what we value?
   - How can we work toward success under this new definition?
   - How will we support each other as we strive to be successful?

Focus on one question at a time, and be willing to take one to two hours to fully discuss the two main questions as well as the myriad of follow-up questions that will relate to the larger topic. Throughout the discussion, dig deeper into team members' responses, encourage team members to challenge one another, and try to uncover why team members believe what they say. See if you can get the group to coalesce around one or two ideas. At the end of the discussion, you should have a shared definition of what success means to the group, and of how team members can work together to achieve it.

Adapt: Group Exercise

As you evolve and grow in response to your environment, you adapt. You and your team must continually advance and develop in an effort to stay ahead of changing times and dynamics. Adaptation is healthy and should be welcomed, but sometimes it needs to be guided. In order to successfully adapt, it's first necessary to have clarity about what you are adapting to. This exercise allows you to focus on recent changes that have occurred at various levels of your environment, such as the levels of your team, your organization, your industry, and the country or countries where you do business. iContact, an e-mail marketing software company, noticed more global trends related to sustainability, and the company adapted accordingly. Look more closely at your environment, and work to identify what's happening and how your team can adapt.

The four quadrants shown here represent four different levels of your environment. Quadrants like these can represent any number of environmental levels, ranging from global policy and customer trends to technology and media trends, but the topics shown here are a good place to start a discussion about where adaptations may be necessary. These quadrants offer a framework for a conversation with your team that can help you identify trends and encourage adaptation.

Team Level
- How has our team changed recently?
- What additional changes can we anticipate?

Company Level
- How has our organization changed in the past six months?
- What additional changes can we anticipate?

Industry Level
- How has our industry changed?
- What trends might be anticipated?

Country Level
- What broader changes are occurring in the country or countries where we do business (business climate, government, and so on)?
- What changes can we anticipate?

You can lead a conversation about each of these issues by simply taking one quadrant at a time, asking the questions posed in each quadrant, and encouraging input from all team members. After each quadrant has been discussed, further the conversation with the following two questions:

1. Do we need to modify our processes (focus, skills, and so on) in anticipation of these changes?
2. If so, how?

There may not be significant trends that you need to react to in every quadrant, but this exercise can provide insight into where your group needs to focus in order to continue competing at the highest level. Use the responses to the previous two questions to develop an action plan around these changes. Some adaptations may be simple (for example, acquiring training in a specific area), whereas others may necessitate a more complex strategy (for example, iContact's efforts to build sustainability into the fabric of the organization).

STAGE VI: NURTURING A CULTURE OF EXCELLENCE

The following statements are true of teams at stage VI:

■ They achieve long-term success, are considered dynasties, and continue winning well beyond any early achievements.

- They set goals to advance beyond any singular success.
- They commit to continual learning and development.
- They find ways to innovate and stay on the cutting edge in order to differentiate themselves from competitors.
- They fervently protect an internal culture that quite simply breeds success.
- They stimulate evolution within the culture so as to avoid stagnation.

At this stage, the leader has the following responsibilities:

- To find ways to develop processes that enable the team to continually learn
- To create an environment in which new and innovative ideas are welcomed and not perceived as threats
- To drive and inspire continual innovation
- To maintain awareness of a winning culture within the organization

Although stage VI is technically included in the turnaround process, at this point the actual turnaround has been completed. Stage VI exists because it lays the foundation for continued success through an explicit focus on continual learning, a commitment to innovation, and fervent maintenance of a winning culture. Your team now has a winning culture that needs to be understood and protected. Don't take it lightly. Embrace the fact that sometimes the simple act of learning and innovating can keep your culture moving forward.

Continue Learning and Innovating: Group Exercise (F)

An after-action review (AAR) is a standardized debriefing process developed by the U.S. Army. It guides a group through the assessment of a specific project in an effort to best understand what worked, what didn't, and how the group can improve moving forward. An AAR is built around a dual premise: that no individual leader can have a complete understanding of what occurred during an exercise, project, or battle, and that the perceptions of every team member are valuable in accurately discerning what happened. Through the use of an AAR, team members review what the group intended to accomplish, determine a collective understanding of what actually happened, explore outcomes, and reflect on successes.[1] This process forces a dialogue that raises the consciousness of the group and enhances a shared understanding of where the group has been and where it is going while also providing a forum for group members to collectively share experiences and perceptions. An AAR requires the ability to give and receive honest and candid feedback and, ideally, occurs throughout a project (that is, from the planning stage through the action

[1] M. J. Darling and C. S. Parry, "After-Action Reviews: Linking Reflecting and Planning in a Learning Practice," *Reflections* 3:2 (2001), 64–72.

stage to the review process). With the use of an AAR, you catch your team while memories are clear, allow communication to occur as issues are appearing, and engage participants in the outcome.

To run the exercise, begin by posting each of the questions in the following table on a flip chart. As you introduce the exercise to your team, provide some of the basic information about what an AAR is, as just explained. Make sure you emphasize that it is a tool for continuous learning and a process that you and your team will repeatedly go through. Then generate, one at a time, discussions about each of the five questions in the table. As you progress through each step of the AAR, remember to write your answers down.

Step	Question	Purpose	Tips for the Facilitator
1	What was supposed to happen?	This question forces participants to revisit the initial purpose of the action.	At times, it will quickly become clear that there was little clarity around what was supposed to happen. If so, use the questions in step 2 to explore why.
2	What happened? What didn't? Why?	This question explores what actually happened, why it happened, and how it happened. It is essential for the group to be honest about whatever occurred. One way to get at this information is to ask participants to recall key events.	The facilitator needs to work to ensure that all participants are engaged. This may involve posing direct questions to team members, such as "What's one thing that worked? What's one thing that did not?"

Step	Question	Purpose	Tips for the Facilitator
3	What have we learned?	This question begins to explore the gap between the intent (step 1) and what actually occurred (step 2). What lessons lie within? In addition, even if the team executed flawlessly, valuable lessons may have been learned.	This is the most important part of the AAR process: identifying the incremental lessons that were learned during the exercise. Take time to thoroughly discuss this step. No lesson is too small.
4	What do we do now?	The focus of an AAR is action, and this is the point where participants can examine what should be done in the short term, in the middle term, and over the long term. Specific actionable recommendations (SARs) need to be identified.	The SARs need to be as specific as possible. There's a big difference between "We need to increase our call activity" and "Our call activity in the tech sector needs to go from 100 outgoing calls per person to 125 outgoing calls per person. By raising our call activity 25 percent, we'll have a much more realistic opportunity to meet our sales goal."
5	Who else can we tell about what we have learned?	Learning may have occurred within your group, but it will be exponentially more valuable if it is shared with other groups and teams in the organization. Who else will benefit from this newfound knowledge?	Encourage your team to pass this knowledge on to other teams and groups that might find this knowledge beneficial. In passing on the lessons of your team, you are making the entire organization stronger.

Source: Adapted from L. Baird, P. Holland, and S. Deacon, "Learning from Action: Imbedding More Learning into the Performance Fast Enough to Make a Difference," *Organizational Dynamics* 27 (1999), 19–32.

Once you complete the exercise, it can be helpful to reiterate the key points of the conversation and ask if anything was missed. An AAR provides the opportunity for every project to morph into a learning mechanism so that team members can grow stronger as the project advances. Allowing different team members to facilitate the exercise will push emerging leaders to develop new skills while enhancing team communication and chemistry. In this way, an AAR becomes more about the team and can take place even when you are not present.

Understand the Culture: Group Exercise

Edgar Schein defines culture as *artifacts, values,* and *underlying assumptions,* and just as Dan Rooney was fastidious in his efforts to manage and maintain the Pittsburgh Steelers' culture, your team will benefit in better understanding and maintaining its own culture. Here are some questions to help you understand the existing culture in your organization:

1. What are five artifacts (posters, quotes, shirts, and so on) that you can point to in defining your team's culture?
2. What values are underlying those artifacts and the overall culture?
3. What does your culture say about your team? about where it's going? about what it's made of?
4. What can be done to make your culture more explicit and pronounced?

As you continue to move forward, use the answers to the preceding four questions to check in with your team, to ensure that your focus is where it needs to be, and to ensure that your culture supports continuous learning, innovation, and sustainable achievement. Throughout this journey, don't forget how far you and your team have come, and make sure you celebrate the progress.

Notes

Introduction

1. Granholm, J. (2011, June 17). Personal communication.
2. Ibid.
3. Ibid.
4. Ibid.
5. Ibid.
6. Ibid.
7. Ibid.
8. Ibid.
9. Ibid.
10. Ibid.
11. Boyd, L. (2008). "Michigan Ranked One of Best-Managed States in Nation; Recognized For Being Well Managed During Crisis." Available at http://www.michigan.gov/granholm/0,4587,7-168-23442_21974-186671-,00.html (retrieved January 12, 2012).
12. Jacobe, D. (2011). "North Dakota and Washington, D.C., Best Job Markets in 2010." Available at http://www.gallup.com/

poll/146402/North-Dakota-Washington-Best-Job-Market
-2010.aspx (retrieved January 12, 2012).

13. Headapohl, J. (2010). "Granholm Touts Michigan's Progress in Final Radio Address." Available at http://www.mlive.com/jobs/index.ssf/2010/12/granholm_touts_michigans_progress_in_fin.html (retrieved January 12, 2012).

14. Center for Digital Government (2008). "Surveys and Awards." Available at http://www.centerdigitalgov.com/survey/61 (retrieved January 12, 2012).

15. Ibid.

Chapter 1

1. Lencioni, P. (2002). *The Five Dysfunctions of a Team: A Leadership Fable*. San Francisco: Jossey-Bass, 188.

2. Barsade, S. G. (2002). "The Ripple Effect: Emotional Contagion and Its Influence on Group Behavior." *Administrative Science Quarterly*, 47, 644–675.

3. Twerski, A. (1997). *Addictive Thinking: Understanding Self-Deception*, 2nd ed. Center City, Minn.: Hazelden Publishing.

4. Kanter, R. (2003). "Leadership and the Psychology of Turnarounds." *Harvard Business Review*, 81(6), 58–67.

5. Cialdini, R. B. (2004). "The Hidden Costs of Organizational Dishonesty." *MIT Sloan Management Review*, 45(3), 67–73.

6. White, H. C. (2008). *Identity and Control: How Social Formations Emerge*. Princeton, N.J.: Princeton University Press.

7. Seligman, M. P., and Maier, S. F. (1967). "Failure to Escape Traumatic Shock." *Journal of Experimental Psychology*, 74, 1–9.

8. Norman, J. (2010, November 13). "O. C. Manufacturer Enjoys Turnaround." *Orange County Register*. Available at http://jan.ocregister.com/2010/11/13/o-c-manufacturer-enjoys-turnaround/49286 (retrieved January 12, 2012).

9. Hamner, W. C., and Tosi, H. L. (1974). "Relationship of Role Conflict and Role Ambiguity to Job Involvement Measures." *Journal of Applied Psychology*, 59(4), 497–499.

10. Beachamp, M. R., Bray, S. R., Eys, M. A., and Carron, A. V. (2002). "Role Ambiguity, Role Efficacy, and Role Performance: Multidimensional and Mediational Relationships Within Interdependent Sport Teams." *Group Dynamics: Theory, Research, and Practice*, 6(1), 229–242.

11. Rousseau, D. (2004). "Psychological Contracts in the Workplace: Understanding the Ties That Motivate." *Academy of Management Executive*, 18, 1.

Chapter 2

1. Berson, Y., Shamir, B., Avolio, B. J., and Popper, M. (2001). "The Relationship Between Vision Strength, Leadership Style, and Context." *Leadership Quarterly*, 12, 53–73.

2. Lipton, M. (2004). "Walking the Talk (Really!): Why Visions Fail." *Ivey Business Journal*, 68(3), 1–6.

3. Wieseke, J., Ahearne, M., Lam, S., and Van Dick, R. (2009). "The Role of Leaders in Internal Marketing." *Journal of Marketing*, 73, 123–145.

4. Lewis, L. K., Schmisseur, A. M., Stephens, K. K., and Weir, K. E. (2006). "Advice on Communicating During Organizational Change: Content of Popular-Press Books." *Journal of Business Communication*, 43(2), 131–137.

5. Covin, T., and Kilmann, R. (1990). "Participants' Perception of Positive and Negative Influences on Large-Scale Change." *Group & Organization Studies*, 15(2), 233–248.

6. Awamleh, R., and Gardner, W. L. (1999). "Perceptions of Leaders' Charisma and Effectiveness: The Effects of Vision Content, Delivery, and Organizational Performance." *Leadership Quarterly*, 10, 345–373.

7. Kouzes, J. M., and Posner, B. Z. (2010). *The Truth About Leadership: The No-Fads, Heart-of-the-Matter Facts You Need to Know.* San Francisco: Jossey-Bass.

8. Lee, L. (2010, June 8). "An Inside Look at a Business Turnaround." *Bloomberg Businessweek.* Available at http://www.businessweek.com/smallbiz/content/jun2010/sb2010068_954174.htm (retrieved January 18, 2012).

9. Hamel, G. (1996). "Strategy as Revolution." *Harvard Business Review,* 74(4), 69–82.

10. Simpson, D. (1998). "Why Most Strategic Planning Is a Waste of Time and What You Can Do About It." *Long Range Planning,* 31, 476–480.

11. Masicampo, E. J., and Baumeister, R. F. (2011). "Consider It Done! Plan-Making Can Eliminate the Cognitive Effects of Unfulfilled Goals." *Journal of Personality and Social Psychology,* 101(4), 667–683.

12. Gollwitzer, P. (1999). "Implementation Intentions: Strong Effects of Simple Plans." *American Psychologist,* 54(7), 493–503.

13. Bernstein, D. (2010). "Broadway's 'Spider-Man': The Full Story." *Chicago.* Available at http://www.chicagomag.com/Chicago-Magazine/December-2010/Broadways-Spider-Man-The-Full-Story/index.php?cparticle=3&siarticle=2#artanc (retrieved January 18, 2012).

14. Healy, P. (2010, November 28). "'Spider-Man' Takes Off, with Some Bumps." *New York Times.* Available at http://www.nytimes.com/2010/11/29/theater/29spiderman.html (retrieved January 18, 2012).

15. Healy, P. (2011, March 22). "Another 'Spider-Man' Actress Injured." *New York Times.* Available at http://artsbeat.blogs.nytimes.com/2011/03/22/another-spider-man-actress-injured (retrieved January 18, 2012).

16. Locke, E. A., and Latham, G. P. (2002). "Building a Practically Useful Theory of Goal Setting and Task Motivation: A 35-Year Odyssey." *American Psychologist*, 57(9), 705–717.

17. Locke, E. A., and Latham, G. P. (2006). "New Directions in Goal-Setting Theory." *Current Directions in Psychological Science*, 15(5), 265–268.

18. "Broadway Grosses: *Spider-Man: Turn Off the Dark*." (2011). Available at http://www2.broadwayworld.com/grossesshow.cfm?show=SPIDER%2DMAN%20TURN%20OFF%20THE%20DARK (retrieved January 18, 2012).

Chapter 3

1. Davis, D. A., Thomson, M. A., Oxman, A. D., and Haynes, R. B. (1995). "Changing Physician Performance: A Systematic Review of the Effect of Continuing Medical Education Strategies." *JAMA: The Journal of the American Medical Association*, 274(9), 700–705.

2. Edmondson, A. C., Bohmer, R. M., and Pisano, G. P. (2001). "Disrupted Routines: Team Learning and New Technology Implementation in Hospitals." *Administrative Science Quarterly*, 46, 685–716.

3. Edmondson, A. (1999). "Psychological Safety and Learning Behavior in Work Teams." *Administrative Science Quarterly*, 44, 350–383.

4. Kaiser, R. B., Hogan, R., and Craig, S. B. (2008). "Leadership and the Fate of Organizations." *American Psychologist*, 63(2), 96–110.

5. Schein, E. H. (1990). "Organizational Culture." *American Psychologist*, 45(2), 109–119.

6. Schein, E. H. (1992). *Organizational Culture and Leadership* (2nd ed.). San Francisco: Jossey-Bass.

Chapter 4

1. Jackson, S. E., and Dutton, J. E. (1988). "Discerning Threats and Opportunities." *Administrative Science Quarterly*, 33, 370–387.

2. Kovoor-Misra, S. (2009). "Understanding Perceived Organizational Identity During Crisis and Change: A Threat/Opportunity Framework." *Journal of Organizational Change Management*, 22(5), 494–510.

3. Chouinard, Y. (2005). *Let My People Go Surfing: The Education of a Reluctant Businessman*. New York: Penguin, 185–186.

4. Hensley, S., and Stensson, A. (2009). "The Restaurant Industry Outlook Softens as the Restaurant Performance Index Fell to a Record Low In December." News release, National Restaurant Association. Available at http://www.restaurant.org/pressroom/pressrelease/?ID=1734 (retrieved January 26, 2012).

5. Domino's Pizza, Inc. *Domino's Pizza 2008 Annual Report*. Available at http://media.corporate-ir.net/media_files/irol/13/135383/DPZ2008Annual_Fullversion.pdf (retrieved January 26, 2012).

6. Reivich, K., and Shatte, A. (2002). *The Resilience Factor: 7 Essential Skills for Overcoming Life's Inevitable Obstacles*. New York: Random House.

7. Schneider, S. L. (2001). "In Search of Realistic Optimism." *American Psychologist*, 56(3), 250–263.

8. Greenlees, I. A., Graydon, J. K., and Maynard, I. W. (1999). "The Impact of Collective Efficacy Beliefs on Effort and Persistence in a Group Task." *Journal of Sport Sciences*, 17, 151–158.

9. Krueger, N. E., and Dickson, P. R. (1993). "Perceived Self-Efficacy and Perceptions of Opportunity and Threat." *Psychological Reports*, 72, 1235–1240.

10. Krueger, N. E., and Dickson, P. R. (1994). "How Believing in Ourselves Increases Risk Taking: Perceived Self-Efficacy and Opportunity Recognition." *Decision Sciences*, 25(3), 385–400.

Chapter 5

1. Covey, S. R. (2004). *The 7 Habits of Highly Effective People: Powerful Lessons in Personal Change*. New York: Free Press.
2. Winick, J., and Tocchini, G. (2011, August). "The Streets Run Red," part 2: "Exit Strategy." *Batman and Robin, 1*(24B). New York: DC Comics.
3. Friedman, T. L. (2006, December 22). "And the Color of the Year Is." *New York Times*. Available at http://query.nytimes.com/gst/fullpage.html?res=950CE1DE1131F931A15751C1A9609 C8B63 (retrieved January 27, 2012).
4. Certified B Corporation (2011). "What Is a B Corp?" Available at http://www.bcorporation.net/about (retrieved January 27, 2012).
5. Elkington, J. (1994). "Towards the Sustainable Corporation: Win-Win-Win Business Strategies for Sustainable Development." *California Management Review*, 36(2), 90–100.
6. Reeves, M., and Deimler, M. S. (2011). "Adaptability: The New Competitive Advantage." *Harvard Business Review*, 89, 134–141.

Chapter 6

1. Lindsley, D., Brass, D., and Thomas, J. (1995). "Efficacy-Performance Spirals: A Multilevel Perspective." *Academy of Management Review*, 20, 645–698.
2. Office of Communications and Family Outreach (2009). *Seven Keys to College Readiness: A Parent's Resource for Grades K–12*. Rockville, Maryland: Montgomery County Public Schools.

Available at http://www.montgomeryschoolsmd.org/info/keys/documents/sevenkeys.pdf (retrieved January 27, 2012).

3. Dyer, J. H., Gregersen, H. B., and Christensen, C. M. (2009, October). "The Innovator's DNA: Five 'Discovery Skills' Separate True Innovators from the Rest of Us." Harvard Business Review, reprint R0912E.

4. National Football League (2011). *2011 NFL Record and Fact Book*. New York: National Football League. Available at http://static.nfl.com/static/content/public/image/history/pdfs/InsideTheNumbers/Record_Since_Merger_2011.pdf (retrieved January 28, 2012).

5. Mosley, M. (2008, August 29). "NFL's Best Fans? We Gotta Hand It to Steelers (Barely)." Available at http://sports.espn.go.com/nfl/preview08/columns/story?id=3530077 (retrieved January 27, 2012).

6. Schein, E. H. (1990). "Organizational Culture." *American Psychologist*, 45(2), 109–119.

7. Frontiera, J. (2010). "Leadership and Organizational Culture Transformation in Professional Sport." *Journal of Leadership & Organizational Studies*, 17(1), 71–86.

8. Bouchette, E. (2011, January 26). "Steelers Treat IR Players Same As Starters." *Pittsburgh Post-Gazette*. Available at https://plus.sites.post-gazette.com/index.php/pro-sports/steelers/107727-ed-steelers-treat-ir-players-same-as-starters (retrieved January 28, 2012).

9. National Football League (2012). "History: Team Capsules." Available at http://www.nfl.com/history (retrieved January 28, 2012).

10. Schein, E. H. (1992). *Organizational Culture and Leadership* (2nd ed.). San Francisco: Jossey-Bass.

11. Sheridan, P. (2011, July 18). "Patricia Sheridan's breakfast with . . . Dan Rooney." *Pittsburgh Post-Gazette*. Available at http://www.post-gazette.com/pg/11199/1160919-129.stm (retrieved January 28, 2012).

12. Bruno, J. (2010, October 25). "NFL Power Rankings: 50 Greatest NFL Head Coaches of All-Time." Available at http://bleacherreport.com/articles/500844-nfl-history-50-greatest-head-coaches-of-all-time (retrieved January 28, 2012).

13. Kotter, J., and Heskett, J. (1992). *Corporate Culture and Performance*. New York: Free Press.

14. Sarros, J., Gray, J., and Densten, I. (2002). "Leadership and Its Impact on Organizational Culture." *International Journal of Business Studies*, 10(2), 1–26.

15. Miller, I. (2004, September 12). "It's the Rooney Way: Family's Integrity Permeates Steelers." *San Francisco Chronicle*. Available at http://www.sfgate.com/cgi-bin/article.cgi?f=/c/a/2004/09/12/SPGR58NB431.DTL (retrieved January 28, 2012).

Acknowledgments

Both of us, Dan Leidl and Joe Frontiera, would like to extend our heartfelt thanks to everyone who participated in this book. You have our deepest gratitude for supporting this project as well as our respect for you as progressive leaders who are guiding inspiring teams. Thank you! Your stories were inspirational and educational, and they have the potential to help many other teams turn around.

Thank you, Karen Murphy, for the opportunity to write this book. Your confidence and support made the project go.

Thank you, Teresa Hennessy, for your invaluable edits and insights.

Thanks also to the many people along the way who supported and encouraged us. Without Andrea Useem, Lillian Cunningham, John Jilloty, Jack Watson, Lisa DeFrank-Cole, and others who believed in us and gave us a shot, we might never have pursued this project.

Dan would like to thank his beautiful wife, Erin, and his son, Holden, for their constant support and inspiration, as well as his loving parents and his four siblings, who have been behind him all the way.

Joe would like to thank his wife, Megan, and his daughter, Quinn, for carrying him through the day-to-day of family life during this project. He wants to let them know—he's back!

About the Authors

JOE FRONTIERA, Ph.D., is cofounder and managing partner of Meno Consulting, where he works to help leaders and their teams perform at a higher level. Joe coauthors a regular column in the *Washington Post*'s "On Leadership" section and has also been featured in *CLO* magazine, *CIO Insight*, the *SportBusiness Journal*, and the *Journal of Leadership and Organizational Studies*. Joe has survived cancer, three years of Division I Crew, and the WorldCom scandal, and he draws on those experiences to further assist corporate, government, and athletic teams in reaching their potential. In his off time, Joe enjoys playing with his children and the increasingly infrequent opportunities to travel with his wife.

DANIEL LEIDL, Ph.D., is cofounder and managing partner of Meno Consulting, where he works to develop leaders and their teams. In addition, Dan writes and speaks to audiences about creating a positive culture that both motivates and inspires. Dan's interests in leadership and team dynamics developed while he was a lacrosse player and coach, competing collegiately, professionally, and internationally. In his free time, Dan loves watching films, swimming in the ocean, and being a dad. Dedicated to seeing the sport of lacrosse grow in the country of his heritage, Dan sits on the board of the Irish Lacrosse Foundation.

Please visit www.menoconsulting.com for more information, or to contact Joe or Dan.

Index

231